PUBLIC SPEAKING

Influence People Using Powerful Public Speaking and Communication & Social Skills

(Proven Strategies to Overcome Your Fear and Speak With Confidence)

Roger Hale

Published by Rob Miles

© **Roger Hale**

All Rights Reserved

Conversation: Influence People Using Powerful Public Speaking and Communication & Social Skills (Proven Strategies to Overcome Your Fear and Speak With Confidence)

ISBN 978-1-989990-17-9

All rights reserved. No part of this guide may be reproduced in any form without permission in writing from the publisher except in the case of brief quotations embodied in critical articles or reviews.

Legal & Disclaimer

The information contained in this book is not designed to replace or take the place of any form of medicine or professional medical advice. The information in this book has been provided for educational and entertainment purposes only.

The information contained in this book has been compiled from sources deemed reliable, and it is accurate to the best of the Author's knowledge; however, the Author cannot guarantee its accuracy and validity and cannot be held liable for any errors or omissions. Changes are periodically made to this book. You must consult your doctor or get professional medical advice before using any of the suggested remedies, techniques, or information in this book.

Upon using the information contained in this book, you agree to hold harmless the Author from and against any damages, costs, and expenses, including any legal fees potentially resulting from the application of any of the information provided by this guide. This disclaimer applies to any damages or injury caused by the use and application, whether directly or indirectly, of any advice or information presented, whether for breach of contract, tort, negligence, personal injury, criminal intent, or under any other cause of action.

You agree to accept all risks of using the information presented inside this book. You need to consult a professional medical practitioner in order to ensure you are both able and healthy enough to participate in this program.

Table of Contents

INTRODUCTION 1

CHAPTER 1: WHAT IS PUBLIC SPEAKING? 5

CHAPTER 2: WHAT IS PUBLIC SPEAKING? 10

CHAPTER 3: ORGANIZE YOUR THOUGHTS 15

CHAPTER 4: PUBLIC SPEAKING IS EASY... YOUR VOCABULARY CAN MAKE IT HAPPEN! 20

CHAPTER 5: THE POWER OF SILENCE 25

CHAPTER 6: OVERCOMING STAGE FRIGHT 32

CHAPTER 7: DEALING WITH COMMUNICATION APPREHENSION 39

CHAPTER 8: A CONFIDENT SPEAKER 42

CHAPTER 9: GETTING RID OF YOUR CRUTCHES 49

CHAPTER 10: PRACTICE MAKES PERFECT 59

CHAPTER 11: FUN AND LEARNING - A DEEPER CONNECTION 67

CHAPTER 12: VOCALS 72

CHAPTER 13: NOBODY IS PERFECT - MISTAKES ARE GUARANTEED 84

CHAPTER 14: HOW FREE PROFESSIONAL SPEAKING GIGS HELP YOU 94

CHAPTER 15: HOW TO VISUALIZE 105

CHAPTER 16: PREPARING YOURSELF MENTALLY 118

CHAPTER 17: HOW TO TURN ANXIETY INTO EXCITEMENT 128

CHAPTER 18: SPEECH STRUCTURE 135

CHAPTER 19: CREATING YOUR SPEECH 146

CHAPTER 20: BODY LANGUAGE 153

CHAPTER 21: TALK ABOUT SUBJECTS THE AUDIENCE CAN RELATE TO 162

CHAPTER 22: PREPARING YOUR SPEECH 166

CHAPTER 23: WHAT TO SPEAK ABOUT 171

CHAPTER 24: DEALING WITH PROBLEMS 185

CONCLUSION 194

Introduction

It's time to start turning words into money, that is because **each and every one of us can "passionately say something about what we know or love and" thus, earn a living out of it!** And the truth is, you do it on a daily basis either with your family, friends or loved ones!

You talk about football, sport, entertainment, business, education, love, relationship, fashion etc. And sadly, each time you do so **you have no faintest idea that you're wasting money-making ideas!**

And yes, without any misconstrue you can speak what you know and make honest, 5 to 6 figure income out of it!

So with this book, . . .

You're Just One Step Away From Speaking Words That Can Be Turn Into MONEY With The Opportunity To Be Interviewed,

Appearing On Radio and TV, And Earning a Living From Speaking What You KNOW!

The Simple Guide to Effective Public Speaking! will help you get into yourself to bring out that sleeping but **salable ideas** which you can use to generate massive income for yourself!
It is a practical book intended to show people on how to . . .

1. How to get into yourself to bring out that sleeping but salable ideas which you can use to generate an annual and massive 6-figure passive income online and move from being broke, massively being in debt and living a life of quiet desperation!
2. The secret to overcoming self-doubt, low self-esteem and fear than you've ever thought possible to building self-confidence, self-control, self-discipline, self-love, and maximizing your social skills, conquer resistance, break through limitation and become unstoppable.

3. A workable game plan on how to have an all-inclusive exotic press trips speaking on what you know.

4. A proven step-by-step strategy to start appearing regularly in lifestyle and in-flight magazines.

5. Opportunity to be interviewed, appearing on radio and TV – but most of all, earning a living from speaking what you know.

6.Speaking powerful, exciting and inspiring words that can be turn into money.

This book is written for Lay Men and Women like yourself; for Politicians, Businessmen, Lawyers, Public Speakers, Religious Leaders, Entrepreneurs, Company Agents, Sales Personels, PROs, Media Houses, Journalists, Writers and anyone willing to take up a leadership position that demands speaking to the public.

Hence anyone who wants to build the power of their spoken words, win over a debate, convince their opponent, make others to do their bidding, and run a successful speaking campaign, engagement or seminar can benefit from this book.

After reading this infectious book, you will have a great understanding and confidence on how to speak to anyone to do your bidding and desire regardless of status or clause, or to run what you know as a speaking business.

It deals with all the aspect of becoming a proficient, successful, public speaker.

Chapter 1: What Is Public Speaking?

We, humans, are special because we have the ability to communicate with each other through language. Communication comes in many forms. Usually, we communicate with just one person. Often times, we communicate with a small group of peoples, such as our family and circle of friends. On special occasions, we are obliged to speak in public, whether we want it or not.

Public speaking is the coordinated and structured manner of speaking to a group of people, which is usually composed of a large number of audiences. Public speaking is done in many aspects of life. At school, the teacher may require you to do a report on a particular lesson. During graduation day, an achiever is required to deliver his or her graduation speech. When the elections are approaching, electoral candidates are obliged to speak in public for their campaign speeches. People do public speaking during business reports, at thanksgiving parties, when making announcements, at wakes, at weddings, and a lot more.

Public speaking is categorized according to its purpose. It may be informative, persuasive, or entertaining.

Informative public speaking aims to inform. The purpose of a public speaker who delivers an informative speech is to share knowledge to his or her audience, an example of which is speaking in a business seminar. The speaker, informs his or her audience about how a business runs, how it can affect your living, what the risks and challenges are, and many more. It does not necessarily have to persuade the audience to start a particular kind of business, nor does it have to be entertaining. The sole purpose of the speech is to impart knowledge on a particular subject to an audience. Speakers commonly use informative public speaking, because they only need to relay the information to the audience.

Another type of public speaking is persuasive public speaking. When you are about to graduate high school, a number of representatives from different universities visit your school. They talk to you and to your batch mates about the benefits and advantages that you can get when you choose to enroll in their universities. They begin presenting to you data and statistics that say how better their performance is as compared to others. They tell you reasons why you should choose their school and not others. These kinds of speakers aim to persuade. By the end of their speeches, they expect at least a number of people from their audience to believe them and make them do the things that they want their audience to do, like for example, purchase the product that they are endorsing. Persuasive public speaking requires extra effort because aside from credibility, it demands conviction and sound argument. Poor argumentation leads to failure of achieving the ends of persuasive public speaking.

The third type of public speaking is entertaining public speaking. As the name suggests, the goal of this type of public speaking is to entertain. It aims to provide humor to its audience. The mood of this type of speech is usually light. The topic may be serious, but delivered in a humorous or entertaining manner. By the end of the speech, the audience will be cheerful, energetic, and satisfied. This type of public speaking is usually reserved for welcoming remarks, weddings, thanksgiving ceremonies, and other not so serious events. Entertaining public speaking may seem easy to deliver, but it actually requires additional effort. The speaker must possess a humorous and entertaining character in order for him or her to be an effective one.

Knowing the different types of public speeches according to purpose is necessary in preparing and conducting your speeches. This will help you to know what characteristics you must possess so that you will become an effective public speaker. In the next chapter, you will know that importance of public speaking. You will be informed of the reasons why public speaking is necessary, as well as the benefits that set it apart from other kinds of speeches.

Chapter 2: What Is Public Speaking?

Leadership requires good public speaking skills

Public speaking, as a form of communication, has been formally defined as the process of speaking to a group of people in a structured deliberate manner. This is generally understood as being face-to-face speaking between a speaker and a crowd or group of people. The objective of each speaker will, of course, be different but most commonly it will be to inform, motivate, influence or simply entertain an audience. And indeed throughout history public speaking has been used as a tool to inspire and motivate the masses. Regardless of its purpose, the skill of public speaking is a very useful and powerful tool in both personal and professional life. Public speaking is a necessity for those in public life. Those involved in management and leadership, for example, cannot avoid public speeches. Therefore, excellent communication and public speaking skills are essential for success. These skills are not only essential for success in leadership and management, they are also essential for anyone seeking career progression or for the individual's own private development. But leaders and managers must be effective public speakers in order to get their message across. So, the ability to speak well before a group of people or a crowd is an essential social skill.It is no coincidence that people who have gained notoriety or fame are almost always excellent public speakers.They are usually successful and influential people because of their mastery of the art of public speaking.

Some of the most famous people in history, and infamous ones, of whom I am sure a few will spring to mind, have used their public speaking powers and verbal rhetoric to captivate their listeners and win people over to their point of view. One such famous public speaker was the American civil rights leader, Martin Luther King, Jnr., whose powerful and inspirational 'I Have a Dream' speech, in the 1960s, captivated and galvanised people around the world. It's still a source of inspiration for many to this day because of the potency of its verbal rhetoric.

Dr. Martin Luther King -
American Civil Rights Public
Speaker

Winston Churchill, former British Prime Minister - was a powerful and effective public speaker during the Second World War

However, many are effective public speakers because they have learned to master the art of public speaking, through training and experience. Most will have gone through a process of training, have had a lot of practice and opportunities to perfect their public speaking skills, and so were able to overcome any public speaking fears. On the other hand, the vast majority of people may only ever have to speak in public on very few occasions during their lifetime: and having to do so without the benefit of experience or training. It is no surprise then that so many people have that fear of speaking in public. But, avoiding public speaking at all cost is not the solution: it's necessary to confront the fear and conquer it. Fear of speaking in public will then be a thing of the past. It will then be possible to become an effective public speaker. And one can only begin to overcome fear of speaking in public by realising that it does not have to be a stressful experience.

Chapter 3: Organize Your Thoughts

Next, it's time for you to organize your thoughts!

Sure, it sounds like a cliché, but it's true: An unorganized mind won't be able to produce viable results simply because it in itself is already confused. Your audience doesn't know what's in your mind—that's true. But, that does not mean that you can just allow them to see that you do not know what you are talking about, you have not practiced well, and that you're not confident enough to be onstage.

Make an Outline

Here's the thing: Whether in writing or in speaking, outlines matter. People often forget to organize their thoughts logically, and thus, when they present their ideas to an audience, the audience feels that it's all cluttered. It's so hard to make a point when your ideas are cluttered!

You know, you can actually make use of cue cards even in impromptu speeches. This is because it's always better to present your thoughts in a clear and coherent manner, instead of jumping from one topic to another.

Get some cue cards (i.e**., index cards, notebook/notepad pages**, etc.) and make an outline of the topic you've been given.

Here's an example:

Main Topic: Today's Music and How Much it has changed

Outline:

Brief History of Music

Artists who are on top of their careers today

The biggest difference between yesterday and today's music

Is today's music entertaining?

Pros and Cons of today's music

How music could still evolve

After making an outline, you could just look at the cue card and focus on one item at a time, instead of say, talking about how music has evolved, talking about its history, and jumping to differences between yesterday and today's music. You have to start from the beginning, and then just let your ideas branch out. Having an outline will also prevent you from using fillers and having dead air, which could definitely make anyone feel bored.

Think of a Diamond

Wait, what?

Okay, in case you're confused right now, let me clarify this for you. A Diamond starts with a point that could then expand to another point, and end in a close. A diamond is perfectly shaped—it's not like a circle that just goes on and on. In short, when you begin to form your thoughts as a diamond, you get to start with a strong point, make valid arguments, and you'd then get to close your speech in a strong and plausible manner.

In short, make sure that you get your audience's attention right away. One good way of doing this is by asking a question.

For example:

Quick: Have you heard about the recent growth in the number of mass shootings in America? Crazy, isn't it?

See, with that kind of question, you already get to create sense of urgency, plus you also get the audience to think because you have just asked about an important matter—something that concerns everyone. Thus, it becomes easier to expound—it becomes easier to evoke people's emotions and make sure that they're listening to you.

Make use of examples and arguments

The thing about public speaking is that it doesn't have to be verbatim. You can make use of examples related to what you have in your outline. You can make use of arguments, and of course, you could also ask your audience some questions.

It's all about making sure that everyone is involved. For example, say that **One Direction** may be today's **The Beatles**. See how your audience reacts—and then expound on what you said. It's also important to be well-read so that you could use a lot of examples, and really help your audience understand what you are talking about.

Know What You're Talking About
Just like what I have just said, it's essential for you to know what you're talking about instead of making your audience feel like you're as clueless as them. Also, make sure that after expounding on the topic, you still get to narrow your thoughts down to a coherent conclusion. This way, people won't get confused, and would really be able to understand what your point is. Make sure you leave them with either a question, or a call-to-action. This way, you'd also feel good about your speech— and will not be scared anymore the next time.

Chapter 4: Public Speaking Is Easy… Your Vocabulary Can Make It Happen!

Do you remember in the previous chapter I asked you to seek out the definition of the word 'vocabulary'?

In this chapter it becomes most useful. Sometimes oneofthebiggestfearsthatpersonshaveabout publicspeakingisnotbeingabletousetheright words to convey the precise meaning. If you wrote this down as one of your fears then this is one sure way to overcome that fear. Build your vocabulary.

HOW DO YOU BUILD A HEALTHY VOCABULARY?

By studying the dictionary? By spending 24 hours a day in the library? By going back to grade school and learning new words all over again?

It need not be so tedious. A word a day keeps your word bank in credit and happy!!

Words are the tools of speech. Notice how often the average person uses the word "nice" to describe any number of things and situations – "He is nice", "the drink is nice", "that's a nice dress", "it is a nice day", "it was a nice party" and so on.

Now let's look at the difference when the word 'nice' is substituted with other words to express a more apt description relative to the situation-

"He was most hospitable"

"The drink has a delicious flavour" "The dress is quite trendy"

"The party was exceptionally enjoyable"

"The day is marvelous"

These examples are quite simple but make the point.

We build a good vocabulary by first making the decision to do so. Automatically the subconscious tunes in to the intention and before you know it everywhere you turn new words stand at attention for your admission into your word bank.

Reading widely is the most highly recommended method for your human mainframe computer (the brain) to build its database of words, their contextual use and pronunciations.Reading for your degree or your work does not count, as it is limited to your area of study or occupation.The human mind becomes excited with novelty – reading articles or magazines or books – fiction as well as non-fiction will inform you of new and useful words for your speech utterances when you least expect.

If you do not usually read Popular Mechanics magazine – do so every now and then – your mechanic might be surprised! And it is guaranteed you will find a new word.

If you deliberately learn ten (10) new words and their definitions each week, no matter the origin of your words by the end of twelve months you would have invested 520 words into your vocabulary bank...think of how verbally rich you would feel.

Make the commitment to learn 10 new words this week —It will definitely help improve your speaking skills.Write down 10 new words every week in your notebook.You are invited to write even more than 10 words per week in your notebook.

EXERCISE:

How many other words could you substitute for the words "to get"?

Target: 40 words

Here are a few to get you started:

obtain, arrest, understand, earn, accept, inherit, acquire

(See answer page for an extended list)

I invite to also complete the next exercise – it will test your vocabulary and show you that your vocabulary is probably better than you think!If not, then you need to do the work of building your vocabulary!

EXERCISE:

Synonyms are words that have similar meanings.

Without consultingyour dictionary,find a synonym for the following words:-

Behavior-child-conflict-copy-group-prime

Write the synonyms in your notebook.

Once you have done the exercise then go ahead to use your dictionary to check the accuracy of the words you selected.

The point of this exercise is to show you your own understanding of words, already existing in your vocabulary.

Once you check and improve your vocabulary on a weekly basis you will find that your base knowledge of words, their meanings and contexts opens up a new creative world for you. You will discover that your opinions begin to surface even more, new thoughts and ideas occur to you, a new awareness begins to develop.

Make the commitment today to allow your vocabulary to contribute to your becoming an effective public speaker.

Chapter 5: The Power Of Silence

There goes a saying that no man ever made a fool of himself who kept his mouth shut.

Now, some of you might well be scratching your heads. Advice about staying silent? When we're discussing **public speaking?**

Believe it or not, yes, silence actually does have value even in public speaking. It's for the same reason there exist spaces between words when they're written.

A whole mass of letters jumbled up together isn't going to make a lot of sense, any more than a whole mass of words just blurted out with barely any pause for breath in between. Silence can be of great value when it comes to speaking publicly, if properly applied.

Let's start with a basic technique, here. Don't speak too fast. The audience might not be capable of following your words if too closely strung together, especially if they're unfamiliar with your mode of speech or your accent.

Instead, keep things slow, and keep things calm. That'll add a nice bit of gravitas to your speech, which is not to be scoffed at.

Whenever you hesitate, take advantage of it: turn it into a pause and say to yourself a few short words of encouragement: "God save the King", maybe, or "I can do this", or "Keep it rocking".

This'll let you remember what you wanted to say next, and keep you bucked up to boot.

Now, unless you're specifically aiming to leave the audience exhausted and dazed, give them a few longer pauses here and there to let your words sink in.

There may be times that a speech is used to batter at an audience's emotions, but that's a rather advanced tactic better left to experienced speakers, and it'd take a natural at public speaking to manage it in his early days.

If you've got visual aids out, it may be better to let the images speak for themselves. Give them only enough for some context, but don't insult their intelligence by explaining everything, not unless it's absolutely necessary.

And after all, the saying goes that a picture's worth a thousand words, so let their minds put the words in for you — there's less work for you that way.

There's also the matter of choreography. Yes, I said choreography. You won't need to dance on stage, but it's certainly worth mapping out your movements when you're up there.

This is why it's best to scope out your location before you get started, and see where the audience will be seated. Find that spot on stage where everyone can hear you equally, mark it in your mind, and center yourself around it.

That's where you ought to start things, and where you ought to keep yourself for most of the speech.

Movement plays as much a role in public speaking as your words, and they don't take a lot of extra effort. Move away from your marked center spot to emphasise certain things, or bring a few words closer to this sector of the audience.

It might be a bit difficult to make eye contact with someone distant, so move closer and then meet her eyes – that'll work and draw their attention, if they weren't looking already.

Most importantly, **never turn your back on the audience.** Showing them your backside is going to break whatever connection you had with them, and it's going to be a bit before you regain it.

If you've got any presentations, then familiarise yourself with the layout beforehand so you won't need to turn your back. People should always be in front of a speaker, and not behind.

Just because you're not speaking doesn't mean you're not doing anything. Often, it's what isn't said, and what doesn't need to be said, that can help things along.

The Duck Rule

The saying goes that, if it looks like a duck, quacks like a duck, and walks like a duck, then it must therefore be a duck. This can be used to your advantage.

Let's get started on thinking like a duck, as that may well be most important. Clear your mind of every thought that touches on fear and nervousness.

Instead, think of something along the lines of: "I'm going to speak well." "I'm going to give them a good speech." "The audience is going to like this speech." "The audience will think that this is the Best Speech Ever." And so on, both for yourself and for the audience.

Thinking about how afraid you are and how you're going to screw up **will** make you afraid and get you screwing up, so eliminate those. Nine-tenths of the battle is in the mind, and a man unwilling to fight has already lost half of the war.

Make sure to keep thinking like a duck as we get you moving like a duck. Don't let the arms hang; else the shakes are just going to collect there if they do.

Move them around a little, use them to emphasise points and illustrate your words. Pointing may be rude in most cases, but giving someone the pointer finger in a speech is sometimes effective. The same advice goes for your legs.

Walk a little bit, and get them loosened out. Standing still may well get the shakes collecting in your legs, and it's rather hard to look dignified if your legs are trembling like mad.

Don't speak with any tense muscles; loosen them out before you start speaking, and keep up a bit of motion while you're at it. You're not delivering a recorded speech, and you certainly aren't a record player with a human exterior.

Thinking and moving like a duck's good, so now we get to acting like a duck. The most important detail in such is a phrase that many British people will be familiar with: "Keep Calm and Carry On." It's been stated before, yes, but it can't be stressed enough: Never under any circumstances let the fright show.

There's an audience out there watching you, do you want them to see you're wracked by the fright? No, so best keep it inside. No matter what happens, **keep it inside.**

To reinforce the above, **smile**. Think of something nice, something happy. There's not much sense in feeling down before a performance, and even less so for a speech – the audience doesn't like it when their speaker's tired and overwrought.

It might be called public **speaking**, but posture and gestures convey as much as words will. Put a smile on your face, keep your back straight, and speak calmly and clearly – now, there's someone acting like a duck.

So, you're thinking, moving, and acting like a duck now – who's to say you aren't, in fact, prepared to give a speech? So, get your chin up, get your smile on, and walk on that stage, and **rock it.**

Chapter 6: Overcoming Stage Fright

When we were kids, the Boogeyman lived in the basement. As adults, the Boogeyman is on stage and he is just as scary. I developed my fear for stage when I was probably 9 years old. It was a school play and I was a tree. And just like a tree, I was shaking and I was not trying to emulate the tree perfectly. I was scared. It was so bad that I ended up falling down and taking the whole cast with me. That is not something you recover from easily. In retrospect, it is hilarious. But at that point in time, it was hell. Even to this day, I still have this tiny feeling that when I get on stage, I am going to trip and fall and takedown anyone who is on stage with me. So, when you see me get up there, I am usually extra cautious with my movement. I count my steps. I try to have fun but at the back of my mind that feeling is there. And that is what fear is at the end of the day... a feeling.

In the right setting and in the right context, fear is a biological instinct that alerts you to danger in your environment. If there is a threat to your person, fear is what kicks in to help activate your survival instincts. So, if you look at it this way, fear isn't really bad. However, when an incident occurs that allows you to live through some kind of trauma, fear registers this incident on your brain. The purpose of this is to anticipate events so that even before they happen, your survival instincts will kick in to preserve you. Except that this time around, the event itself that triggered that that fear in the first place has not happened, but your brain has read certain signals in your environment and interpreted it as 'this event is imminent'. So, it sends a message to the rest of your body saying 'protect yourself'.

Let us imagine the scenario where a girl went hikingin the woods. This is her normal route.every time she gets the chance, she takes aslow stroll in nature.

She enjoys the pleasures of nature and basks in it. Then one day, on one of her hiking trips, she hears a rustle of leaves. She turns around and sees nothing but she senses for steps behind her. She turns again and says nothing. And just as she turns to resume her journey, someone jumps out from the bushes and pounces on her. Somehow, she is able to itfight off her attacker and escape.This is a traumatic experience for her and even though she bravely fought off whoever attacked her, her brain is not going to focus on her bravery rather it would register the incident.

In the likely eventthat her passion for nature is stronger than her fear from the experience, she would put aside her fears and start hiking. However, even if she chooses a different location for her hikes, every time she hears the rustle of leaves, panic and fear will immediately set in. This is exactly how fear works. It takes an experience, builds on it and then activates your instinct every time your brain reads signals in your environment that bear any similarity to that experience. Sometimes, we don't even have to experience that incident personally. Some of our fears are based on second-hand experiences. When people tells us a horrific story or maybe you heard something scary on the news, these nuggets of information are fed to your brain and the fear that you felt in those moments are registered. So then anytime you detect signals that are close to those experiences, you are immediately put on alert. This process applies to stage fright as well. You get on stage and immediately your body is put in survival mode. The last thing you are thinking of is the speech you are about to give and all you want to do is escape.

To overcome this fear you would need to retrain your brain and this starts with simple exercises that you can carry out daily. These exercises would give your brain new signals and help you focus on what is real as opposed to what is perceived in order to retrain your brain.

Step One

Identify and isolate your fears. It doesn't matter how irrational they may sound. If they cause you to feel fear, put them on the list. You can take things a step further by asking yourself what exactly it is you are afraid of.When it comes to stage fright,the common fear is the fear of judgement. We feel that the people we are speaking to are judging us. And when you look at the specifics of it, you'll find that things like our physical appearance, perhaps our diction/accent as well as our personal storiesare some of the things that makes us feel insecure. Be as specific as possible in this process.

Step Two

When you recognise those things, the next step is to take action. One of the things that helped me on my journey is affirmations. positive affirmations are a way of self-reprogramming with the use words.these words help to affirm the positive truths about you so that you can stop focusing on those negatives that make you feel insecure there are so many articles on the subject of positive affirmationsand their impact on our overall mental health.

Step Three

The final step here is to change your perspective. When we have traumatic experiences whether personal or second-hand, we tend to focus on the negatives. In fact, we go as far as building a future of possibilities with those negatives. In order to change your perspective, you would need to change how you think about that situation. And to do this, your focus has to be drawn to the positives. If we revisit the example I gaveearlier, the positive there was the fact that the lady was strong enough to fight off her attacker. No matter how bad a situation is, there are positives. Look for it and hold on to it. By changing your perspective, you force your brain to create a new narrative. So, where the stage was seen as where the Boogeyman is, you begin to see stage as where your opportunity is.

Task:

Do a research on positive affirmations. Find phrases that resonates deeply with you and then create your own list of 10 positive affirmations that you will be speaking to yourself daily. If you have had any negative experience that has traumatized you and is preventing you from getting on stage, the focus here would be to look on the positive side. Write out three positives that came out ofthat experience starting with the fact that you are a survivor and for that alone you are a victor and not a victim.

Chapter 7: Dealing With Communication Apprehension

I'm reluctant to spend too much time sharing how people get nervous about public speaking. Sometimes I think students of public speaking get nervous just thinking about how speaking in public can make them nervous.

Remember that you have an important message for your audience!Just knowing that you have material and information that they may not get anywhere else should be plenty of motivation to push back the fears and share your message with gusto.

Even with this positive mantra, however, many of us get butterflies –often depending on what audience we are speaking to—when we need to speak in public.

A word of advice about public speaking --- relax.No one expects you to step up to the microphone or podium or wherever you are speaking and be the best orator of all time.Most audiences expect you to be a little nervous.Let yourself be a little nervous.In fact, those nerves will work for you.They are **facilitative** because they facilitate your good performance.The kind of nerves that can stop you in your tracks are **debilitative**.They prevent you from doing a good job.

First and foremost, put your presentation in perspective.When a speaker is nervous I often ask:**Why are you nervous about this?What is the worst thing that can happen?**

Some tips to reduce your nervousness:

Prepare well

Practice

Bust a move – yes, exercise!I know it seems like odd advice, but simply moving around physically may help you release much tension that could creep into your public speaking.If you are toward the end of a group of speakers speaking on one day, be sure to get up and move around a few minutes before you speak if you can.Sometimes just sitting there "stewing" about your upcoming speech can make you even more nervous.

Chapter 8: A Confident Speaker

To think that you can be good public speaker without confidence is like jumping off a cliff without a parachute!

Confidence is the most essential element in public speaking; everything else takes a back seat. If you put a confident bloke on stage who doesn't know a dime of what he needs to speak; he will do far better than the guy who knows everything but is pretty short in confidence. Stage speaking is more about confidence than anything else.

How do you gain the ability to believe in yourself and to demonstrate that belief to the whole world? Do you always have to feel confident to look confident? And is reducing anxiety the same thing as gaining confidence?

Another important thing is not to think about the result. The moment you worry about the result you are letting anxiety creep into your system. The result is the greatest source of anxiety in life. But why worry about the result; if you are just normal and act like it's just another day in your life - you will do great.

Another way of being a good public speaker is to believe that you know more than the audience. This might seem arrogant to the 'gurus' of public speaking but it has worked for me. By thinking the audience knows lesser than what you know you get confident and words start to flow smoothly from your mouth.

First of all, what does confidence look like? A confident speaker exudes positive energy that feeds and excites the audience. A confident speaker appears strong and authoritative, but not intimidating. A confident speaker appears relaxed but not sloppy, positive but not saccharine, and knowledgeable but not arrogant.

There are obviously different ways to learn how to be confident in Public speaking. I have seen people speak in front of a mirror to gauge how well they are doing, is the body language correct, etc. Majority of people like to do mock presentations to select group of audience to check out the reaction. Whichever way you try; you need to be confident on your d-day. But beware of over-confidence. You ought to have some butterfly's in your stomach. That will keep our feet rooted to the ground.

Confidence is both mental and physical. It's the positive way you perceive yourself, and it's the way your body projects that positive self image. Here are some strategies to move toward both the mental and physical expression of confidence.

Always be Prepared

You must be well prepared in order to feel confident. That means you're speaking about a topic you believe in, you know your topic inside and out, you've organized your thoughts into a cohesive presentation, and you've practiced it enough not to be thrown off by unexpected questions or mishaps. "Winging it" or tossing together your presentation the day before it's due is only going to increase any anxiety you have about speaking.

Preparation means visiting the venue where you'll be speaking to get a feel for the room, the layout, where people will be sitting, how much you'll have to project your voice, and how intimate or formal the setting will be. Where will your equipment go? Where will you stand? Feeling comfortable in the space where you're speaking will increase your confidence.

Preparation also means anticipating distractions or mishaps. Plan ahead for computer glitches, hostile audience members, forgetting your place, a waiter dropping a plate, and any other problem that might arise. Anticipating mishaps is not the same as worrying about them. When you've got Plan B and Plan C in place, you can actually relax more, because you know you're ready for anything.

Embrace Your Uniqueness and Imperfections

A confident speaker doesn't worry about what the audience thinks of her. A confident speaker is more concerned with delivering value and meeting the audience's needs. So what if you have a lisp, a visible tattoo or a hearing impairment? So what if you have a Scottish accent, a booming voice or you're from the projects? Make the most of your uniqueness, stand out from the crowd, and be proud of who you are!

If you have a strong accent, slow down when you speak and get feedback on your presentation before you deliver it to make sure you can be understood. If you have a booming voice, make sure to use vocal variation, and be sensitive to the size of the room and how close the audience is to you. The point is this: make your uniqueness work for you, not against you. Never be ashamed or embarrassed about who you are.

Audiences don't want speakers who are perfect, by the way. They want to be able to relate to and connect with the speaker.

A presenter who is perfect makes her achievements seem unattainable. Be human, be real, and be you.

Use positive self-talk to reframe the way you perceive yourself as a person and a speaker. Before your presentation, say to yourself, "I believe in myself," or "I'm special and unique, and there's no one in the world like me." It seems a little corny, but affirmations work! Pair your mental practice with physical practice. Make sure your posture, eye contact and body language also say "I'm confident."

Don't Apologize

A confident speaker doesn't let the audience know when he's nervous. What? Confident speakers get nervous? Yes, of course they do!

The difference between a confident speaker and one who lacks confidence is that the latter tries to gain favor with the audience by pointing out or apologizing for his nervousness. This doesn't gain points with the audience; in fact, it makes them pity the poor speaker. A confident speaker doesn't want pity; he wants respect! A confident speaker appears calm and relaxed, even when nervous. This takes physical and mental practice, but the pros do it every day and so can you.

When things go wrong in your presentation, don't dwell on them and don't announce them. The audience most likely has no idea that you've lost your place or left something out. Keep going as though nothing has happened; the show must go on.

In the event that you make an obvious mistake, like spilling your water all over the lectern, take care of the problem quickly, lighten up the situation with a little humor, then move on. If you dwell on it, so will the audience. Successfully and smoothly handling a mishap shows you're a professional and adds to the audience's positive perception of you.

Chapter 9: Getting Rid Of Your Crutches

What are crutches? Those annoying things that hurt your underarms and help you get around after you have broken a foot or leg. Crutches are the same with speakers ... only they annoy your audience more.

How many times have you been distracted by watching a speaker:

- Hold onto the podium till their knuckles turned white.
- Stay in what I call the "Buffer Zone"—the speaker takes one little tiny step away from the podium but never veers out of arm's reach so he can grab onto that podium as if it's going to save him.
- Walk across the stage in a straight line with his shoulder facing the audience because he likes talking to the sidewalls.
- Look above the audience's heads or dart his eyes back and forth across the

audience so as not to look anyone directly in the eye.

- Keep his/her hands folded in front, plays with a ring, continually puts a hand in a pocket.

- Say "ah, and ah, umm, soooo, you know, you know"? How many times have you started counting with your fingers or making little tick marks on your paper when you've heard someone do that?

All of these are crutches. What do crutches do? They appear to help you when you think you need help. What does a crutch do if you always use it? It becomes a crutch.

You'll never walk until you get rid of the crutches.

I can hear you saying, "How do we let go of the podium? My notes are there and I'll forget what I'm going to say." Remember what we said in Chapter 1: Talk about something you know well, something you are passionate about. You know how you feel about something, you KNOW the story you want to tell, because it's something

YOU have experienced ... take those sections and totally remove yourself from the podium. The faster you remove yourself from the podium, the faster you will never use it again. Don't fool yourself by staying in the Buffer Zone either, that's not really letting go of the podium.

Talk about something you know well, something you are passionate about.

Another crutch is looking above the audience's heads, talking to the back wall; talk to your **audience** not to the back wall. It really amuses me when I see a speaker talk to the back wall because some other speaker told them, "It's okay if you don't look directly at the audience because that is the best way to start out speaking if you're too nervous." This myth in speaking comes from acting where it **is** used. Remember the fourth wall? Actors are taught not to break the fourth wall by looking above the audience's heads, to look at a fixture on the wall or down the aisles, so as not to look directly at the audience. That's the difference.

Speakers don't have a fourth wall; speakers should make eye contact with their audience. Remember what we covered about eye contact in Chapter 2—Fearlessness. If you have improvement to make in this area, start developing that eye contact in everyday conversations. When you do, you will soon feel more comfortable making eye contact with everyone you meet, including your audience.

Now, what is it about those hands? What is it that makes people not know what to do with their hands? Guilty, guilty, guilty … coming from a Greek family you learn, like the Italians, you have to talk with your arms and hands and find your arms flailing all over the place. If you could have seen me when I first started acting, you'd be laughing. My gestures looked like one of those giant gumby-like balloons on a windy day. Or maybe you're the opposite: the praying hands person, the ring twirler or the pocket man.

These are some of the most common crutches when starting out in speaking.

Okay, story time again. Another acting story and, yes, I was a hot mess when I started acting. My gestures were all over the place ... meaningless and they didn't connect to what I was saying. I felt like my arms and hands always needed to be moving in order to express myself. I thought I was being dramatic.

Then one day my acting professor in a very stern voice told me, "NIKKI, PUT YOUR HANDS IN YOUR POCKETS" I looked at her like, "You're kidding, I've got to use my hands." "PUT YOUR HANDS IN YOUR POCKETS, NOW!" She made me practice a monologue like that for days on end, until one day she said, "Only bring your hands out of your pockets when you connect with what you are saying." Here I thought I was being dramatic when all I was doing was being an actor being an actor. It wasn't like magic ... it took time and practice ...until I finally changed my flailing habit. I began to realize that my gestures needed to connect with what I was saying and feeling and this is so true with speaking too. Connect to what you are saying. Because if you are not connecting to your own words and feelings how can you possibly connect with your audience?

...if you are not connecting to your own words and feelings how can you possibly connect with your audience?

As I am rereading this before going to print, I am reminded of a speaker who I saw live just a couple of weeks ago. Now granted the speaker makes money because they have an unusual niche but I truly wonder if what this speaker says goes home in a doggy bag with their audiences. The overt over-acting of emotions was so melodramatic that you could see the audience tune the speaker out after just a few minutes. There was no real connection with what the speaker was saying to what they had experienced. The speaker was pushing themselves and the message on the audience and they didn't realize how much more effective they could be if they would just be real.

It takes practice to get your body, arms and hands to work for you and not against you.

It takes practice to get your body, arms and hands to work for you and not against you. Take the time to feel your words and eventually your gestures will begin to flow and become natural to you.

The best way to begin your descent from flailing arms and hands, praying hands, ring twirling or being a pocket man is in everyday life.

We have to create new good habits for a strong stage presence.

First, set your mind to break the old habit, then when you catch yourself using this old habit in everyday life, make an immediate mental note of what you are doing and let your hands drop slowly to your sides. Yes, it feels uncomfortable at first letting your hands sit by your sides, but that will change. Like making eye contact ... if you start changing these habits in your everyday life, they will come to the speaking stage with you.

You have to get your subconscious mind to take it all in. Your subconscious mind is that place where things become second nature to you. Like getting a glass of water. We don't think, "Oh, I have to get a glass out of the cupboard, I must grip it so it doesn't fall out of my hand, then I have to turn on the water." It's second nature to us.

When you finally get to the point of not thinking about what to do with your hands, you'll have one less thing to worry about...your gestures will flow more naturally. Just like getting a glass of water, you feel the thirst and that feeling brings on the natural gesture of getting that glass of water.

It's the same with the "ahs, and ahs, uhmms, the sooo's and you knows." Set your mind to break the habit. When you catch yourself saying the filler words, say to yourself, I just did it again and keep trying to stop yourself, even if you are in the middle of a "YOU KNOW" and correct it immediately. Instead of saying, "You know, you know, what I'm trying to get across?" Stop yourself right in the middle of those "you knows." Then ask yourself, "What can I say instead?" Correct yourself and speak it out loud. You might then say, "Do you **understand** what I'm trying to get across?

Eventually, you'll get rid of all those fillers. But trust me they do sneak in from time to time even with the best of speakers.

Most importantly don't beat yourself up— keep working on creating new good habits. Remember new habits can be formed in just twenty-one days but it takes about three months for them to become second nature to you.

In summary:
Get rid of your crutches.
Make immediate mental notes about useless gestures and hand movements.
Drop your hands to your sides.
Make mental notes about filler words.

Create new good habits.

Chapter 10: Practice Makes Perfect

One of the secrets of a good oral presentation is practice. It is considered the most essential and beneficial preparation before your big day. The more time you commit to practicing, the higher the chance that you will become confident on stage. Through repeated practice, you can easily memorize your speech, recite every detail, practice your hand gestures, and know what to clearly emphasize to your audience. You can time yourself so that the day your actual presentation comes, you will not end up hurrying or underprovide them with what they need.

In a structured presentation wherein you have your introduction, middle, and closing sections, it is more effective if you read through all of them first. Familiarize yourself with its content and order. Once you get familiarized, that's the only time to start to practice it in full form - which means that you get to recite it with vitality and character by incorporating your visual aids, props, and strategies appropriately.

Practice As If You Were On Stage

Practice how you should stand, how you walk, and how you use your gestures. As you practice, make sure that you will also take note of the time. Ensure that your exposure will only be within the given time allotted for you. At this stage, you will be surprised that the presentation will be longer than what you have imagined.

Practice as if you were talking to your audience. By doing this, you can talk to yourself in the mirror. Practicing facing a mirror is by far the best tactic used by successful people. Through this method you will have a reflection of yourself, looking at how your gesture and reactions will be when presenting. Though it is funny seeing your own self while practicing, you can trust me that it works a wonder. Lastly, take note of your facial expressions, and smile appropriately.

Ask a tactful but honest friend to watch you practice. Ask for an evaluation on how you can improve. Allow them to critic your body language, your tone and volume of voice, and your pacing. Ask whether they can grasp or understand what you want to imply. Taking into account the feedback you received, it is now time to refine your presentation. Rehearse again with all the changes; ask for some criticism and refine your presentation until you are satisfied.

Words to Ponder

If you have a video camera, you can use it to record your rehearsals. Review your records every time after your practices to know the things that you need to improve and maintain. Know the points where you are taking too long, or the points where you get lost a bit.

If you are going to use audio-visual equipment, do not take anything for granted. Double check them first and plan for contingencies. Ensure that they work and ask on how to control or manage them, so you will know how to control them by the time of your actual presentation.

Also, ensure that the planned room will provide an ideal environment for listening. Make sure that the room's capacity is big enough to accommodate the audience and activities that you have planned.

What Does your Body Tell

Aside from spoken words, your body and movements relay mixed messages that are often misinterpreted by your audience. Your body speaks what it has been feeling in a way your tongue never does. Therefore, here is a list of common body languages you should be aware of, and movements you should get rid of.

1.Hand Movements

Don't: Presenters commonly commit mistakes in terms of how they would use their hands to blend with their speech. One would know if a presenter is nervous if he or she clasps his or her hands, hides them from behind, or fidgets them. Those hand movements may also mean that you are not firm or confident enough about what you are saying. Hands on pockets indicate that the presenter is afraid, uncertain, or disinterested in his or her own presentation. In addition, it may also appear rude to some. Your audience's attentiveness lies also on how you would show them your confidence on the piece that you are presenting.

Crossing of arms is another hand mistake that the presenters should avoid. It indicates that he or she is not enthusiastic about the presentation. It is considered as a defensive posture that shows resistance which creates a gap between you and the audience.

Do: Therefore, to look confident, you must keep your arms open and in front like giving a bear hug. Such welcoming and engaging open hand movement will relay a message of peace and confidence to the audience. Use your hands appropriately in a concise and orderly manner to emphasize your point.

2. Eye Contact

Don't: It appears to be very facetious and unprofessional when you do not lay your eyes onto the people you are talking to. Looking at your watch may be disrespectful. It could mean you are bored and you want to end this thing quickly. In addition, looking at your feet or ceiling indicates nervousness.

Do: Instead, make eye contact with your audience especially when you are emphasizing a point. Don't look at your audience in a threatening way. Just show that what you are saying is true, essential, and meaningful. Look at different audience and spot for those that are attentive to your presentation and maintain eye contact with them for a few minutes. This would indicate that you impart knowledge or the information you imply in a passionate way.

3. Posture

Don't: Limping your neck and slouching your back and shoulders may convey that you are unenthusiastic and unprofessional.

Do: Sit firmly or stand tall. Maintain a neutral position. Standing is the most preferred posture and with a straight posture, you are actually creating a very professional impression on the audience.

4. Legs Movement

Don't: Jiggling legs may signal that you are restless and uncomfortable. Do not walk around the room as if you are conducting some practical lesson or performing arts in the circles.

Do: Stand comfortably. You may step a few steps forward when projecting some useful information while presenting. You may also move to your left or right where the screen is projected to pin-point some important information. Other than that, control your movement.

5. Facial Expression

Don't: Your facial expression provides a long lasting impression on the audience. Do not forget to smile but do it in a non-threatening way.

Do: Smile naturally. Nothing beats the positivity that a smile could radiate.

People will accept your speech more willingly if it is accompanied with a smile. Your audience will smile back at you which could lighten your mood up.

Words to Ponder

Keep calm and maintain composure. Your body can tell your audience if you are not confident or unprepared for your presentation. Be wary of your movements. Stage presence is always important.

Chapter 11: Fun And Learning - A Deeper Connection

For 15 years I've taught trainers and leaders and instructional designers the significance of making any learning event more fun. I've given them reasons and ways to do it. I've written about it many times including
All of the things I've taught and techniques I've used are valuable and helpful.
And they aren't enough.
The training techniques and ideas all concentrate on the learning procedure. And whilst the procedure is essential; when we focus too closely on a procedure we could lose view of the result.
It is like whenever you tell somebody their form is wrong and ignore that they still out bowl you by 30 pins. Or whenever you tell somebody they hold the pen wrong when they write, but they still have pretty handwriting. Or they seem to do something in an unconventional but

successful way.
In all of these cases, the concentrate on procedure keeps our view away from the wanted result.

So it is with fun and learning.

Will our learning be deeper and more lasting (as well as more pleasurable) if we do things to make the procedure fun? Obviously.
But as I already stated, that isn't enough. If the person leading the training doesn't

comprehend why those techniques work, or believe that they will work, they will just be "using techniques" and it's going to feel just like that to both the teacher and the student. It's going to be like putting a band-aid over a wound far too big - helpful maybe, but not truly a solution. So what's the deeper connection?

The Deeper Connection Between Fun and Learning

It is basic. The result of learning is:

- Satisfaction
- Happiness
- Success
- New skills
- Greater self-confidence
- More security
- Enjoyment
- Fun

The result of our learning something new is supposed to be fun. This fact is largely why the techniques work - they are putting the procedure of learning in alignment with a deep human truth. When we learn we are expressing a deep human need and exercising our greatness. When we learn we are doing what we know subconsciously we are supposed to be doing. And when we put our decisions in alignment with those needs, it makes us joyful. The result of learning is deep fun, enjoyment and satisfaction. Too usually we forget this - both as students and as teachers. Learning is fun. Maybe this chapter assists you comprehend why the greatest trainers seem to make the learning procedure fun and engaging. Maybe now you comprehend why you use those types of ideas. Maybe you even see ways you could teach coworkers, peers and your kids things more efficiently.

I hope so. But my real hope in sharing this with you is that you think about your personalized experiences and beliefs about learning.

This deeper connection between learning and fun matters to us - and not just since we may be educating somebody else - but simply because we are learners too.

And we'll be more efficient learners, more productive learners and more successful in our lives when we recapture the joy and yes, fun that inherently comes from learning new things.

Chapter 12: Vocals

Making the Most of Your Voice

Vocal dynamics aren't just important tools for singers and actors. It's easy to think that as a speaker or presenter, the quality of your voice is at most secondary to the information you are getting across, but performers see them as equally important. The most interesting speech in the world will have little impact is spoken without purpose, and on the other hand the most vocally impressive speaker will fall short if their message is insignificant.

Essentially, you need both. An interesting speech, and the ability to get it across effectively, and a huge part of that relies on your vocal skills. The exercises in this section are designed to help you achieve your potential vocally, by working on pacing, vocal inflection and appropriate vocal projection.

Speaking Out

Three things contribute to dynamic vocals, and will be discussed on the following pages:

Breathing: as speech is produced by exhaled air passing over your vocal folds and through the mouth. The work in the *Breathing* section is a great starting point for this, and this section develops from that and looks at the effect breathing has on the pace of your speech.

Inflection: understanding vocal inflection helps you avoid monotonous speaking (a listener's nightmare). It also helps you to put the right stresses on the right words so you can add colour to your speech.

Projection: learning how to speak at the right volume for the size and distance of the audience, and the size of the room you're in. Also learning the difference between projection and shouting.

1. Slow It Down, Breathe Through It

Most people are understandably scared of speaking in public, and naturally can't wait for it to be over. This leads them to speak really quickly, and when this is at such a speed that the listeners can't hear each word properly, we call it *gabbling*.

Nobody wants to be a gabbler, and it can be avoided very easily. Just slow it down! If you're aiming to sound empathetic and conversational, think of it as relaxed chat and use the speech pattern you would use *in conversation*. If your objective is to sound concise and informative, slow your speech down to bring emphasis to the important point you are trying to make. If you gabble, you'll sound like you have no confidence in the words that are coming out of your mouth, and you'll look like you want to get out as soon as possible.

You can practice speaking in a well-paced style by doing this:

Print out the text you have to present, in clear large font that's easy to read, and with wide spacing between lines.

Read down the speech as fast as you possibly can - comically fast. Breathe all over the place and get to the end as quickly as possible. This will make you aware of gabbling, and help you remember how to avoid it, by doing it. Think of it as speeding in your car, and give yourself a mental speeding ticket at the end of it.

Read the speech again, but slow it down and lengthen out pauses. You should sound more relaxed and confident, with a higher status.

Mark on your speech with an 'x' each time you take an in-breath. This helps you to pace yourself better and your breaths should decrease in frequency and stretch out for longer the more you practice and use the exercises in the *Breathing* section.

2. Verbal Crutches
"Um... Uh... Like... Y'Know... eeer...Basically..." Most of us guilty of this! We don't even realise it, because we do it all the time, but "Um's" and "Ah's" crop up all over the place, as we use them to fill a gap while we think, or to keep our listeners attention while we check our notes. We call them *Verbal Crutches*

because we use them as a lifeline of support, but they *always* have the *opposite* effect we want.

To raise your awareness of your own use of Verbal Crutches, and to help eradicate them, try this:

Recite the story of your day so far, from the moment you wake up, in as much detail as you want (don't use a printed speech as you probably won't "Um' and "Ah" if reading from the page). The first time you do it, put in as many Verbal Crutches as you can, in places where you might usually put them. E.g. "I uh, got up and uh got out of uh, bed, and basically started uh, getting dressed y'know…"

Recite the story of what you did yesterday, and this time do it in your normal conversational style. Notice if you use any Verbal Crutches.

Recite what you will do tomorrow, but in the manner you would use when speaking in public or presenting. Make a conscious effort to use no Verbal Crutches at all, and if you do, make a mental not of why you used one at that particular point.

If you're extra conscious you can even use cognitive learning on yourself, where you give yourself a little pinch each time you use a Verbal Crutch!

3. Master the Pause

The best actors and the best public speakers/presenters have something in common: they all know how to manipulate pauses. Done in the right place and for the right duration, a pause can have an unprecedented effect. They can give gravitas to your speech, help build anticipation, and make your listeners hang on your every word. It's ironic how sometimes, the most powerful thing you can do with your voice, is nothing.

So what's the secret to mastering the pause? Look at your speech - it's right there. It's called punctuation. Full stops and commas, question marks and colons, they're everywhere, so use them! Here's how:

Get your printed script and circle every full stop and question/exclamation mark in one colour, and every comma or colon/semicolon in another. You should have made rather a mess of your paper.

Read through the speech, pausing for 2 whole seconds after each full stop or question/exclamation mark, and 1 second after each comma or colon/semicolon. Hear the added impact as you get to the end of each point, and remember the feeling. Sometimes it feels right, sometimes it feels wrong, it's up to you to find the most poignant places to pause, and when to move on.

Remember
Pausing helps you to collect your thoughts, gives your audience an opportunity to digest your information, helps to get rid of Verbal Crutches and gives impact and variety to your message.

4. Inflections

Vocal inflections are the stresses that we put on particular words to give them emphasis. We do it in everyday life (e.g. "I saw this HUGE cat"), and it helps us to add colour to the stories we tell.

People often assume that when they're speaking in a professional environment that you have to lose this colour, but it really isn't the case. Speaking without any inflection is desperately dull to listen to. If you want to make people engage with your words, you have to make them interesting somehow, and adding inflections is the way to do it.

Add inflections simply by taking your printed speech and underlining the words and phrases you want to give particular emphasis to. Ration them wisely as people who use too much inflection tend to sound irritating. A common mistake for instance is when you hear someone go higher pitched at the end of every sentence as though it's a question. It's equivalent to this book having question marks instead of full stops - not very pleasant for anyone.

5. Record Yourself
By far the easiest way to monitor and improve your vocal dynamics is to record yourself speaking. Use a dictaphone, laptop, phone, anything with an inbuilt microphone, and practice your speech to it.

Notice any uneasy breathing, any Verbal Crutches you use, any opportunities for pauses that you misses, and any badly placed inflections. Get someone else to listen too - it can be hard to judge yourself with an unbiased or uncritical ear.

Know The Room, Know Your Audience
Projecting your voice appropriately relies on your ability to perceive the size of the room and the audience, and the distance of the audience from you.

Your voice carries differently in different rooms. If the room is small, you might get away with speaking just above normal volume, and you will find it easier to sound conversational. If the room is bigger, like a court room or large office space, you will need to project and push your voice from your diaphragm.

Similarly with audience size, if you are speaking to only a handful of people, they should be able to hear you okay. But if you're delivering your speech to a crowd, you'll have to speak louder and in a strong voice to assert your status.

Plan ahead and find out about the room and the audience size before you go to speak, or you might be taken by surprise!

6. Projection Practice

The aim of this exercise is to raise your awareness of projection, and to remind you of the need to project appropriately for the size and distance of the audience you will be speaking to.

Projection isn't about shouting, it's about gauging from merely looking at a performance space the level and volume you will have to pitch your voice for the whole audience to be able to hear you, without over-doing it and deafening everyone on the front row.

It takes a lot of practice in a lot of differently sized spaces to be able to do this, but you can practice by starting small. You'll need to have a line of text memorised, something you can say in one breath:

Hold your hand out in front of you with your finger pointing upwards, as far away from your chest as possible.

Speak your line of text just to your finger, so that if it were a person, it would be the only thing around that could hear you.

Bring your finger half way towards your mouth and do the same, speaking at half the volume.

Bring your finger so that it almost touches your lips and do the same, (this will be barely audible).

Speak the line to an object about 3 meters away from you. Alter your volume and pitch to the exact point the object is at.

Speak the line to the furthest point away from you in the room, without shouting.

Speak the line to all of the different distances at random. Keep repeating the line and changing the speaking destination, and also change at random points midway through the line.

Chapter 13: Nobody Is Perfect - Mistakes Are Guaranteed

If you have been striving for perfection in anything, then I am afraid I will have to be the bearer of shocking news; there is no such thing as perfection. You are trying to catch smoke in a net. You have got more chance of finding a unicorn riding a T-Rex than of finding or creating something truly perfect.

Seriously, perfection does not actually exist on any level which is practically useful to us in our everyday lives. We as humans certainly cannot achieve glorious perfection on anything other than a coarse level of measurement.

If you are finding yourself failing to finish tasks or projects on time, or even at all, because you are always trying to make them better and better you are likely to be a perfectionist. If you find yourself striving to get things exactly right before you proceed then you are likely to be a perfectionist. If you are great at setting project goals and taking initial action but poor at finishing things off because you keep on polishing them before the big reveal, then you are likely to be a perfectionist.

If you are exhibiting perfectionist traits you are not alone; it is a big problem for many people.

Who am I to criticise? I have been a perfectionist myself many times myself. I have bogged myself down in all sorts of ways, especially when writing. I am now constantly on my guard against the demon of perfection.

If you cannot ever get a speech or presentation rehearsed and finished you are going to approach the deadline with less than full belief in your material and nowhere near enough practice under your belt. Is this situation going to be good for reducing your speaking nerves? No way.

As a professional coach I have worked with many people who could not get things finished. Many people say they are trying their best to please others and this is what drives their perfectionism. If something is not perfect, they will worry others will be disappointed with an inferior result, output or idea. The question often asked is, "Is it not only right and proper you strive to provide the best output you can for the intended recipients of your efforts?" Yes, it is and notice the question asked about the "best output you can" and not a "perfect output." Trying to get something perfect for the benefit of others is laudable but ultimately misguided. What is not laudable, however, is the real result of this never achieved perfection. The perfectionist never provides anything at all. No one wins.

Claiming perfectionism is for other people's benefit is an out and out excuse. It is a rationalisation. It is a convenient way of transferring blame onto the unachievable goal of perfection when there is a real root cause much nearer to home. It is a way for the perfectionist to cover up the deeper fears they have inside them.

Extreme perfectionism is an example of a combined type one and type two fear combined. The perfectionist has fears and concerns about their own ability which are coupled with fears about the thoughts and judgements of others. A perfect storm of fear in fact.

So, what about you? If you find yourself tending towards being a perfectionist, what is it you worry about? Do you fear failure? Do you fear success? Do you expect perfection in others? Do you believe they expect it of you?

Here is a reality check for you. If what you have to offer or say is valued and valuable; people will value it for its own sake and not because it is worked, edited or polished to near perfection. To them it is what it is. So, pour your passion and love into your creations and ideas and get them as good as practicable but make sure you stop polishing and get them out there so people will hear them, value them and love them likewise.

There is a law called "The Law of Diminishing Returns" which states in summary, beyond a certain point you get far less improvement in something relative to the amount of work invested to make the improvement. To put it more simply, once you get something as good as you reasonably can then more work will not make any noticeable difference to you or to anyone else.

Remember this, other people are not perfect either.

Most of the time, the things you may see as potential defects and shortcomings will not even be noticed by anyone else. You also have no control over the things other people think and do anyway so why worry about it? Seek feedback and correct things later if necessary.

It is not going to happen overnight, but it will not happen at all unless you start right now. Once you begin to let go of any perfectionist traits you have about speaking and presenting you will naturally worry less and have fewer speaking nerves. You will also tend to speak more often and become a better speaker as a result. Another virtuous circle.

Perfection or relaxation? I know which I always choose nowadays.

Now that we have cleared that up, here is another potentially shocking revelation for you.

You will make mistakes.

Sorry to be the bearer of more unwelcome news but this is also a cast iron fact and there is no getting away from it.

We all make mistakes from time to time. If you ever try anything new you will almost certainly make some mistakes along the new path. The only guarantee I know of for avoiding mistakes is to do absolutely nothing in your life and try nothing new. Ever. That last one is not a good option is it?

It is the same with speaking. You will make mistakes. You will forget words, lines and even whole sections. You will move too much or too little. You will target your material a little too high or a little too low for your audience. You may even create mistakes nobody else has ever made, but you will make mistakes of some kind.

Mistakes are a way of life so make them, accept them, learn from them and then move on.

Usually any mistakes you will make will be small ones, you know the kind which we know about but no-one else notices and with no actual harm done. Occasionally you will make real big mistakes. Real show stopping doozies everyone seems to know about. There is nowhere to hide. You must hold your hands up, take the heat and secretly hope someone else has an even bigger disaster to take attention away from you. Be honest, we have all been there have we not? It cannot just be me.

Here is the thing, whenever we make any sort of mistake it is natural to think about it and run an internal dialogue to review it. A post event personal de-brief if you like.

This analysis can be pessimistic or optimistic. Optimistic is way better.

Instead of looking at what happened during the event and seeing ongoing disaster and negativity, try focusing first on what went well then looking at areas for improvement which will make it even better next time. It is all about using different internal language. Remember we talked about controlling your inner voice in the previous chapter? This is where the rubber hits the road.

Here is the key takeaway phrase. Do not beat yourself up about mistakes. Be kinder to yourself and cut yourself some slack. Practice some self-compassion. It is okay to make mistakes. The real problem comes when you do not learn from your mistakes and you keep making the same ones repeatedly.

Finally, please be aware once again, this type of turnaround thinking takes practice, effort and dedication but once you start to "get it in the muscle" you will see your commitment provides clear and positive results.

Chapter action points

Take some quiet time to examine your relationship with perfection. Only you will know the answers to these questions so be as honest as possible. Identify any concerns you have because you must acknowledge and accept things before you can move on. Whenever you identify any fears or worries, always remember to be kind to yourself and applaud yourself for being such a unique, honest and self-aware human being.

What valuable work or innovative ideas are you holding onto because they are not "perfect" enough for you? You now know the answer so quit seeking perfection and get your work out there, warts and all. You can always alter it later based on feedback.

Work on putting firm preparatory phase cut-off and project completion targets into your plans to help you overcome any perfectionist tendencies you may have.

Think back to the last few mistakes you made in any aspect of your life. How did you analyse the situations at the time?

Were you pessimistic or optimistic in your thinking? How much help did your inner voice give you?

Keep working on your inner voice because it can be a slippery character. Your inner voice, which is your own subconscious by the way, ought to be working on your team so get it on side and keep it there. It is your voice so take control of it.

Chapter 14: How Free Professional Speaking Gigs Help You

One of the primary reasons people get into this business is because they want to earn some serious cash. With dreams of stardom and hopes of owning the Mercedes and the million dollar home, they set off in pursuit of getting highly paid gigs only to get knocked down by rejection after rejection. After doing some research they find that most of their starting events will be free speaking events. What?

If "free" is a horrendous four letter word in your career vocabulary, you'll need to learn the importance and value that "free" can really provide. There are tremendous benefits that come with speaking for free including having the ability to promote your back of the room products where you can actually profit. You'll be gaining new experiences and building your clientele list.

1. "Free" still gets your name out there. The more people who hear you speak, the more people there will be to purchase your product and refer you to other people are looking for professional speakers. For example, speaking for free for an organization like a Rotary Club or Elks Club can lead to paying jobs because many of the members who belong to this organization have businesses of their own or are in positions in their careers where they are the decision makers to "hire" speakers.

2. You can still have the opportunity to sell your products at these free speaking engagements. Statistics show that back of the room products account for over 50% of professional speaking profits. Promote your business and promote your products in the same place! At the very least, you will be able to refer them to your website for more information or additionally, to purchase products and books. The more people that hear you, the more opportunities you'll have.

3. Free speaking opportunities are still opportunities where you can create a video tape of yourself. Many speaker bureaus and meeting planners will not hire you without seeing a video tape of your presentation. On top of that, many organizations like the Rotary Club or Elks Club have people who can help you create your video. Can you trade services?

4. Free speaking engagements are a great place to network. Hopefully by now you understand that you have to get your name out there. In order to get your name out there, you'll have to be out there. You can still mingle with your audience as well as network with meeting planners for the function.

5. A free speaking event is still a great reason to send out a press release. If you're looking for a reason to send out press releases about yourself or your career, use free speaking engagements. Submit them to local newspapers and various online sites that have a 'to-do in

your area" section. This is just another way to get the word out about your business.

Speaking for free has its benefits. What you'll need to learn next is how to leverage these free events into referrals and product sales. As you do this, more people will know about you and your business will be well on its way to success!

If You Like Them, They Will Like You

When you see experienced public speakers, sometimes it seems they can cast a spell on an audience. You as an audience member know what that spell feels like. And one of the first evidences that this public speaker was going to keep this audience in the palm of his hand is that you almost instinctively liked him or her. And the interesting thing about that 'spell" is that once you genuinely like this speaker, you naturally are open to his presentation, you listen more attentively and you are more open to suggestion if the speaker is driving to a point.

So as you prepare to begin doing some public speaking, its natural to want to know how to make that spell work for you. We all have a natural feeling of insecurity or inferiority and we worry that the audience will not like us and our presentation will go badly. So you wonder if that speaker just naturally more likeable than you or did he use some public speaking magic to make the audience like him.

The answer is twofold. First, no, that public speaker is not more likeable than you. That is just your insecurity talking to you and you need to tell that insecurity to take a hike because it is not going to do you a bit of good becoming a better public speaker. And secondly, yes there is something that public speaker knows to make his or her audience like them but no, it isn't magic at all. It is something anyone who stands in front of a crowd can use and it will work every time.

The secret really isn't very complicated at all. You just have to learn to like the audience. That may seem simple but buried in that idea is a powerful principle of psychology. When you step in front of a crowd and you have trained yourself to like them, it comes out in every aspect of your posture and the way you behave. You will smile more, make eye contact and actually find yourself wanting to interact with them during the course of your presentation.

Now don't be concerned if your speech or presentation is not interactive in a dialog sort of way. But if you have spoken to a small group before, you know that there is a lot of interaction going on even during a one way speech. That speaker who charmed you that day with that 'magic" knows that interaction goes on all the time. As you speak, you get feedback in the form of body language and facial expressions that let you know how you are doing. And by starting out with a fundamental warmth and affectionate relationship with an audience, that feedback is warm and affectionate as well and that only makes the presentation more of a success.

The trick to learning to like your audience lies in looking for good reasons to like them. We use the word 'trick" for a good reason.' Any reason to like them will do. You don't have to like every individual in the audience. You might like the clothing they are wearing or the faces of individuals in the audience. You might like certain ones you know or a few you met and found a chemistry with early on. You can even like a crowd just because you find a few in that group attractive. By focusing on the ones you like, your warmth toward them will spread to the rest of the audience as you speak. Before long you will have that crowd in the palm of your hand and using that magic spell to make your presentation a success. Then you will remember this little 'trick". And you will use it often for public speaking success every time.

10 Tips For Professional Speakers

Put your best foot forward every time! One of the reasons that many people fear taking the podium is because they are afraid of being the focal point of everyone's attention and they don't want to make a fool of themselves. There are several things you can do to "fool-proof" your speaking event so that you present well every single time!

1. Take the time to prepare well for your presentation. Preparation enhances your confidence and it's also an opportunity to refine any weak areas in your presentation.

2. Begin and end your presentation on time. Arriving late to your presentation is simply unprofessional; not to mention that it won't win you any points with your crowd. Also speaking over time shows your audience that you don't value their time.

3. Know your audience. The only way you can really relate your audience is if you know who they are. Profile your audience. Are they male or female? What income bracket are they in? Why would they attend your presentation?

4. Dress appropriately for your audience. Not all speaking engagements require a business suit! There are many places where business casual attire has become the norm. Before your audience even hears your message, they are already sizing you up and this is impacting whether or not they are hearing what you have to say!

5. Have a backup plan for visual aids used in your presentation. You've selected to use visual aids because you thought they would be helpful in getting your message across. What happens when laptops fail or the room cannot accommodate presentation equipment? Create a plan on how you would handle a situation like that.

6. Tone down information overload. Yes, you can overload your audience with too much information and if you're not careful, you'll lose them. They'll mentally check out. As a speaker, you'll want to present enough information that hooks them into getting more information from you!

7. Don't use inappropriate humor. Humor can be a tricky thing working for you or against you. You will really have to know your audience in order to use jokes or humor appropriately.

8. Vary your speech tones. The monotonous speaker will lose their audience within the first 15 minutes. It's okay to be animated during your presentation and in fact, doing so will transmit flair and passion that keeps people engaged in your message.

9. Relate your topic back to your audience. Basically, stop talking about yourself! Your audience might want to hear a testimony or two, but mostly, they'll want to hear

about them and how your presentation can help them!

10. Solidify your message. Support your ideas with data and evidence and build a solid case for your viewpoints. You can use statistics, testimonies, demonstrations, pictures and more!

Your presentation can be fool proof if you take the time to minimize mistakes. By going through these key points, you can assure yourself that you are well prepared for any challenge that might come your way and you will experience the success you've always dreamed of!

Chapter 15: How To Visualize

We now discuss the most important part of this audiobook, which is enabling you to perform creative visualization and use it for the achievement of your goals. As you read these steps, remember to be in an attitude of optimism and open-mindedness. Be proactive in writing down your own ideas and avoid all sorts of negative thoughts and doubts in your mind. Find a suitable place for reading, away from various distractions so that you thoroughly focus on reading and try to apply each of the steps if you have the chance.

1. **Narrow down which goal you wish to attain using visualization.** Narrowing down your goals means you have to make them very specific. Of course, you can always start with general ideas. For instance, you can come up with something like "obtain a job promotion." Of course, although this goal is quite specific, you can further narrow it down to better visualize

a fitting mental image by which it can be achieved. For instance, you have to ask yourself questions like, "What would it take for me to achieve a promotion? What should I first be able to accomplish?" With these questions in mind, you will then come up with a clearer picture of how your promotion will unfold, step by step. Consider imagining scenarios that will lead to your promotion such as:

a. Every morning, you come to work looking your best. Your shoes are well polished. You look sharp in your clothes and you have the perfect hairstyle. You come on time and you look absolutely ready for work.

b. You obtain the respect and admiration of your colleagues and your boss because of your stellar performance: your reports are timely, you deliver good insights during meetings and you exceed sales expectations. People say that you are creative, and your colleagues appreciate the job that you do and always wish to be working on the same project as you.

c. Remember that account which no one seems to be able to close? You close it within a week when you make that phone call and office visit to the owner.

d. By the end of the month, your boss takes notice of your stellar performance. He hears about it from various people inside and outside the organization. He calls you to his room and delivers the good news - you are the new sales manager and you get a salary increase. You smile and thank him for giving you the job you've always wanted and deserved. As you can see, you can go through specific mental images that will lead to your success, narrowing down each scenario to what each and every day might look like. Your visualization can even be more specific so that you recall or imagine how your office looks like, name which officemates you get to talk to and so on.

2. **Sit alone in a quiet, comfortable place where you will be uninterrupted.** The importance of being able to focus completely cannot be understated. Here

are some pointers on being at the right place at the right time during your creative visualization exercises:

a. **The importance of being alone.** During creative visualization, you need to be comfortable in the fact that you will be spending some time alone. Being alone enables you to perform intrapersonal or self-communication, and is useful in assessing the issues in your life that are most meaningful to you.

b. **Be in a comfortable place.** A comfortable place is an area where you feel most secure. If you decide to stay in your room, keep it as clean and organized as possible, and lock the door if you have to so that you will be certain that you will not be disturbed. As creative visualization may take some time, it is also important that you find a suitable place where your mind and body will feel relaxed.

c. **Ensure that you are uninterrupted.** It may be helpful to inform your family (or friends if you live in a dorm) not to disturb you for a couple of minutes for your creative visualization exercise. Remember, the key is to eliminate all negative energies and focus on only positive ones. If you are interrupted and you get irritated by the intrusion, you may have difficulty finding a similar mood of peace and balance with which you can start or continue your creative visualization exercise.

3. **Relax.** Both your mind and body must be relaxed during the creative visualization process. This is the reason you have to schedule it, find a place for it and prepare for it. Some methods that work include:

a. **Lying on your back.** This position relaxes your muscles and allows you to completely succumb to the mental images you have prepared to visualize for yourself. Be careful, of course, that you do not fall asleep in the process.

b. **Closing your eyes.** Keeping your eyes closed enables you to come up with a "blank slate," so that you take full control of the environment and setting which you wish to imagine. The items you see in your room or chosen location for the visualization exercise may or may not trigger different kinds of emotions and bring about various kinds of biases. This is why closing your eyes can help you start on a somewhat more neutral ground.

c. **Sitting on a comfy sofa.** If you tend to fall asleep lying down on your back, consider sitting on a comfy sofa while you engage yourself in visualization exercises. This way, you get to practice being comfortable in a good and confident posture, too.

d. **Doing stretches.** Whenever appropriate, do some stretches to further relax yourself and ensure that you are not stressed or are in any way subjected to physical inconvenience. It is important that both your mind and body are at its optimum condition when you are engaging yourself in creative visualization exercises.

4. **Play relaxing music or a prerecorded affirmation message.** Remember how using the different senses of your body can contribute to a strong mental image?

What you hear or listen to greatly contributes to your capacity to succeed in creative visualization.

a. **Relaxing music.** This type of music soothes your mood and relaxes your body. It is ideal to play music that is instrumental in nature, so that you may also verbalize or speak out your thoughts as you engage yourself in visualization. Some great examples of relaxing music to listen to are classical music, piano music from various movie themes and even some violin concertos. If you keep on listening to the same type of music during creative visualization exercises, you will later see that your mind and body will associate this music to visualization exercises so that being in the mood for creative imagination will become easier and more automatic for you. While it is advisable to listen to music, however, be careful if there is anything in the musical selection or playlist that may distract you or remind you of unpleasant memories, as this will affect the quality of your visualization exercise.

b.**Prerecorded affirmation message.** Messages of affirmation are a good way to start and end your creative visualization exercise. You may have someone with a calm, confident and soothing voice read out and record your preferred messages of affirmation, or you may use your own voice. Make sure that the recorded message is of high quality and choose your message of affirmation well.

5. **Visualize a clear and detailed mental image of what you desire to get or accomplish.** When it comes to visualization, clarity and attention to detail are of utmost importance. Besides preparing mental images in correct and logical sequences, important details must not be left out once you have narrowed your goals. Details which you may want to include in your image are as follows:

a. **Persons involved.** Determine the persons who are instrumental to your success. Identify individuals who are likely going to help you. Enable yourself to imagine winning over possible enemies or competition. In your mental image, think about the faces of your allies. Make a very detailed picture of yourself, from what you're wearing to what your face may possibly look like.

b. **Place and environment.** Will you be in school? In the office? At the park? In your car? Determine the location where your visual image is bound to happen. Put various items in place and imagine them too, like the size of the place, where people may be staying, fixtures in the location, equipment you will be using, and so on. Yes, this means that you will include that familiar tree or that elegant desk in your mental image. Why, even the pen you're supposed to use should be in your visualization, too. These things will make it easier for you to relive the actual scenario once you come to face it in real life.

c. **Statements to be said and heard.** What words or statements do you imagine to hear in the process of accomplishing your goal? Do you hear your boss saying "Congratulations" as you say "Thank you" for that big promotion? Do you hear your dream woman saying "Yes" when you propose? Then, include such statements in your creative visualization exercise. You can record these as messages of affirmation or speak them out as you meditate on your visual image.

d. **Specific actions or activities to be engaged in.** Movement is part of your creative visualization process, especially if your goal has something to do with a physical activity like sports or exercise. In your mental image, determine the times when you are likely to stand up, walk, run, or in the context of say, basketball – dribble, make a steal, pass the ball, do a successful jump shot or an immaculate three-pointer.

6. **Have a full experience.** When you are engaged in creative visualization, you do not tell yourself that you are just imagining things. Instead, you let yourself be led to the mental image that you are

creating, making that image your very reality at that very moment. It's like at night, when you're dreaming – you don't really know that you are in a dream, do you? You only find out once you wake up. So, no, you are not supposed to see yourself in your room or in your sofa when you visualize mental images: as you progress with your visualization, you see your physical body being present in the actual scenario you have created for yourself. These can be done through the following:

a. **Use all your senses.** Remember how you're supposed to make a remarkably detailed mental image? This is only possible if you get to use all your senses. You identify what you see around you – you know the colors, the shapes, the brightness of the things that surround you, as if you've went inside a movie. You hear what you're supposed to hear – whether it be laughter, cheering, another person's voice or the sound of your footsteps. If it's all about the woman of your dreams, then by all means, feel free to smell her perfume and touch your hand. Remember, you are taking out all the limits and your mental image can be as real as it can be.

b. **Involve your faith and emotions.** Allow yourself to express your faith and confidence. Verbalize your beliefs and be in touch with your emotions. Do you feel happiness? Then you must be smiling. Do you see success happening? Then you must feel proud. Your mind and body should be one. You will get to feel the emotions which you imagine that you will have.

c. **Feel the energy, as if to have an out of body experience.** Yes, creative visualization is like being transported to a completely different place at some point. It's like allowing yourself to time-travel and go to places and situations you imagine yourself to be in.

7. **Don't ever imagine a negative scenario.** By now, you should realize that you are in full control of your mental image, which is why a negative scenario has no place in it.

There is no reason you shouldn't visualize a positive experience as it is **your** experience. You are the author, so to speak and you will choose to visualize only positive outcomes. There is no place for limited thinking, for doubts, for worries or for anxieties. You design your mental image and every single detail in it is bound to help you become successful. Own up your image – it belongs to you.

Chapter 16: Preparing Yourself Mentally

- I like to say that most things in life are mental. If you can get your head in the right place, you'll do fine. Walking into a situation, psychologically ready to be successful, matters a lot. Good news, we know a variety of things you can do to help prepare yourself mentally to give a good talk. The first important factor we've covered elsewhere that's gaining confidence and mental readiness through proper practice. When you know your material cold, you simply don't worry about it. You experience lower stress the day of the talk and thus you're capable of staying focused.

Your next task is research. The more you understand the people you'll be in front of the less worry you'll experience. I know that many of you speak in front of different types of audiences but in any case, know the basics. Big news in the industry, the company, or with the group, what their culture is like since that might dictate everything from your attire, to your level of detail, and so on. Do your homework. Okay, now I want you to focus on one thing we all know about presentations.

They won't go exactly as you thought they would. Life always throws a few curve balls at you some you'll like and some you won't. Thus it's a good idea to go in expecting something to change or go wrong. Assume the audience is a different size than you expected. Assume the venue will change at the last minute. Assume some type of equipment will malfunction causing you to think on your feet. First, make the choice to laugh at this often unavoidable reality, then decide what you'll do under these conditions and make any necessary preparations before you go to the meeting or event, so you'll be ready.

Next, the night before, get lots of sleep and a quality dinner. This is very serious, don't stay up late rehearsing your presentation. It's too late now, you should have prepared earlier. Don't stay up late with friends socializing, get rested. If you want maximum mental comfort when you step in front of the group you need your physical body to feel as ready as possible. Finally, you need to define and use a solid pregame routine. It might last 10 seconds or 20 minutes, we're all different.

However, to gain focus, confidence, and conviction in the minutes before you present most people find it useful to follow some sort of ritual. For me, before a big speech, I need five minutes alone to play this script over and over in my mind while listening to loud rock and roll in my earbuds. For other people, it's simple, mental imagery imagining themselves giving the speech successfully. For you it might be five minutes of quiet meditation, repeating some affirmation, looking at a picture of your children, or some other ritual that helps you push the stress of the day away.

Check your nerves and get focused and ready to deliver a great presentation. If you don't prepare correctly you'll be a mental mess when it's time to present but it doesn't have to be that way. Follow the practical and simple steps we just outlined and you're very likely to arrive with your head in the game, confident, and ready to look directly at the audience, and deliver a sound presentation.

Imagining your success

- During our discussion of mental preparation, I intentionally skipped one item. Truth be told, there is one tactic that is most important, and that is the proper use of mental imagery, successfully imagining your success. In essence, you'll be engaging a form of mediation that is well known to successful people in many different areas of life, from business to sports to politics. I'll describe the process in a moment, but to start, I want you to plan on doing this at least three times leading up to the presentation.

How long you do this each time is somewhat up to you. Some only need three or four minutes, while others tend to find focus after twenty minutes or more. For me, I do this about one week before a speech, two days before the speech, and the day of the speech as close in time as possible to the actual speech. Through a little experimentation, you'll find your own favorite approach. Now, to begin, of course, you have to try to arrive at the venue feeling healthy, having had adequate rest.

Thus, a feeling of sufficient energy, not hungry or tired. Next, choose the place you wish to mentally prepare. This might be your office, a conference room you know is always empty, a picnic table in the back of the building, or your hotel room, who knows. Based on what's available, find a quiet place that lets you become ready to step up and present. For a few of you, that will involve getting excited or pumped up, much like a weightlifter does before a heavy set, but for most of you, including myself, it will be an exercise in becoming centered, calming your nerves and establishing a sense of peace.

Next, what sounds help you get there? Trial and error will tell you the best answer. It might be no sound at all, through the use of noise canceling headphones, or it could be any form of music that helps you mentally focus on the task at hand. Then, there is the physical position. Is it pacing, standing, sitting or even lying down? We're all different, so try each one and see how you feel. Okay, now when you find comfort with the place, sounds and position, it's time to really think deeply about what you're going to do.

In your mind, I want you to watch yourself deliver the presentation, just like a movie. I want you to imagine success. Do it once very quickly, just to imagine yourself standing there delivering successfully. Then, I want you to get into the details. In that movie playing in your mind, hear yourself reciting the speech word for word. See yourself locking eyes with the audience, watch their positive reactions. See your useful, nonverbal movements.

Take note of your key points, where you really want to add emphasis. See the stage, the screen and your podium if there is one. Imagine success, see yourself really making your points. See positive affirmations and looks of understanding from the audience, see people smiling. It's also really useful to imagine the specific comments and questions you feel are most likely and then see yourself effortlessly and productively respond.

Common sense and good research tell us that if you spend time in some detail envisioning your actual success at a specific task, you will increase the odds of walking into that context and performing successfully. Remember the steps we discussed and you can arrive mentally prepared to deliver.

Reducing the odds of mistakes

- Let's talk about a few easy things you can do to ensure your presentation is as smooth as possible. You've done a lot of preparation and you don't want that to go to waste, so what do you do? Your first task is to always arrive at least one hour before the presentation begins. I know that sometimes that is possible, and other times it's not, but in any case, believe me, the more important the presentation, the more you need to arrive early. If you're ever presenting at an off-site location or a venue you've never seen, it's essential to plan to arrive early, simply due to the possibility of unforeseen traffic problems.

You also want to arrive early because step two is to once again prepare and rehearse. This time at the actual venue. You'll also need to choose where you might place any notes you have, and you can use this time to distribute any handouts to all of the seats. Next, check the audio-visual equipment. Make sure your presentation is loaded long before you're scheduled to begin. Make sure the microphone is working. And make sure you know how to operate the computer or the remote mouse for the computer. In case they somehow misplaced your presentation or the file has become corrupted, always arrive with another copy on a flash drive.

Don't rely on great internet connections that will allow you to pull it from some online repository. Sometimes a connection won't work, so bring a flash drive. Grab some water if you need it and then you're ready for the final rehearsal. Know exactly where you'll stand or pace. Visually go ahead and pick your spots. Stand in front of the chairs, or on the stage, or behind the podium, and start to run through your slides. Barely glance at them, but by now you shouldn't need to. They're just a guide for the audience.

Don't use the microphone, but do say out loud what you wish to say. You can use a hushed tone, but do verbalize what you wish to say. Ideally, you'll get at least one full version of the presentation out of your mouth, nearly verbatim, before the room starts filling up with people. Here's one last useful tip. Think about building rapport with the audience before the talk begins, during the period when people are entering the room. It's time to mingle, instead of staying removed in the front of the room.

Try and think of the two or three people you really want on board when you're presenting. It might be a great idea to go shake hands and say hello when they arrive. Now, I do realize that all of these tips represent an ideal approach to reducing mistakes and delivering effectively, but your goal each time is to do as many as possible to give yourself the best odds of a great presentation.

Chapter 17: How To Turn Anxiety Into Excitement

Before you can put the "excitement principle" into practice, you need to do some preparatory work.The key questions you need to address first are –

Why am I doing this speech/presentation?

Why might this be an exciting opportunity?

What good things might come from doing it?

Only you can answer the above questions because what motivates you may be different from what motivates me or any other person.

In general, giving a presentation to a group of people can lead to a range of positive outcomes such as –

Demonstrating your depth of knowledge on a particular topic to a relevant group of people (such as workmates or others in your field of expertise)

Demonstrating your level of confidence and ability to communicate

Standing out from the crowd.A successful presentation to a group of co-workers and superiors can be the catalyst for advancement within the company or being head-hunted by another company

An opportunity to practice.Each presentation or other public speaking engagement gives you a chance to polish your skills.Public speaking is an art-form, so you can actually use the motivation to become an excellent speaker as your fuel for generating excitement.

The key is working out how to change your filters so what was previously perceived as a threat, is now perceived as an opportunity.

Anxiety winds up due to a feedback loop.There is almost always the following basic process –

Anxiety trigger => Physiological reaction (Increased heart rate, dry mouth etc.) => Anxious thoughts about your physiological state (**"Oh no, I am going to look like a**

fool!") => Increased physiological symptoms of anxiety...and so on.

By changing your filter so that you view your heightened level of arousal as a positive thing (After all, you are just excited!), you short-circuit this feedback loop, keeping physiological arousal to comfortable levels.

Train your amygdala to lose its fear of public speaking

There is one key task you must undertake to guarantee success and it is not something that will come naturally to you (especially if you have been motivated to buy a book such as the one you are reading now), however please bear with me.You have possibly also already encountered this piece of advice elsewhere.However I am going to also tell you **why** this is important.

You need to proactively seek out opportunities to present to groups of people or speak in public.

Did that sentence just put a small knot in your belly?

Here is the reason why this is such a vital component of curing your fear of public speaking.**By actively seeking out the opportunity to speak, you are sending the clear message to your amygdala that there is nothing to fear**.Think about this for a minute.Remember how excitement is an **attractive** motivation whereas anxiety is an **aversive** motivation?And remember how we are reprogramming anxiety as excitement?By actively seeking out speaking opportunities you are reinforcing the message that public speaking is exciting and therefore something **attractive**.

Also, by actively seeking out opportunities to present to groups of people, you also give yourself the ability to harness one of the oldest and most powerful concepts in psychology – **exposure therapy**.As you may already be aware, exposure therapy involves **exposure** to something you fear, but in a controlled way and in a controlled dosage.So, for example, if you had a fear of heights, you would be subjected to gradually increasing heights to slowly reprogram your illogical fear.Perhaps you would start by looking out from the window of a two storey building and gradually work your way up to skyscrapers.Gradually your amygdala becomes confident that heights don't pose any particular threat and your phobia consequently disappears or lessens greatly.

By going out of your way to speak in public, you will be able to initially choose examples which are not particularly stressful and then work your way up in terms of difficulty.The worst possible outcome would be for you to do nothing and then be forced, whether you like it or not, into a huge presentation to a large group of people.Much better would be to actively seek out small, manageable speaking engagements first.Perhaps this could be presenting a work project to your immediate team or some other similarly low-key talk.A suggestion would be to choose a talk that **would** actually be fun or interesting.This will help with your amygdala re-programming endeavours.

Fear of public speaking or anxiety disorder?

One point which needs to be addressed is that of the difference between a fear of public speaking and a more pervasive anxiety disorder.A distinction needs to be drawn between someone who is otherwise untouched by anxiety and someone whose public speaking phobia is indicative of generalised anxiety disorder (GAD), phobic disorder or panic disorder.

The reason why this is important to clarify is that, depending on which of these describes you, a different approach is required.

If your fear of public speaking is a manifestation of an underlying anxiety disorder, you would be best served addressing your broader issues before looking specifically at your fear of public speaking.The benefit of doing this is that you may find, by treating the underlying disorder, you also treat your public speaking phobia. For example, if you decide to go down the pharmacological route (either via SSRI antidepressants, benzodiazepines or other), you may find that by treating the biological underpinning of your current issue, it may resolve naturally. I know of several examples personally of people who lost their fear of public speaking after a period of treatment with SSRIs. On the other hand, if you decide to concentrate on CBT (cognitive behavioural therapy) as a means to address your issues with anxiety, this will also give you valuable techniques for reframing your interpretations of certain events. These skills will stand you in good stead for any efforts to reframe anxiety as excitement.

Chapter 18: Speech Structure

You probably remember from your school days how to write and structure a paper. Well, there is really not that much different for writing your speech or seminar. You start with an introduction, body and conclusion. Before you start writing there are a few things you need to know. Know how much time your speech should take and time that's allotted. If you don't have a time limit, try to keep your presentation brief, yet informative.

Find out about your audience **(reference chapter 5 for more information).** Give a lot of thought about your audience and how best to structure your presentation. This is a very critical step in your speech preparation. If you do not find out about your audience, prior to presentation it could have a negative. Here's an example:

Your presentation in the past is geared for an audience of middle-aged professionals. However, you find out when you get there, your audience is made up of college students. You are now facing a potential generational issue that could very well "tank" your presentation. If nothing more, a delivery style modification is required. If you are fast enough on your feet, you may be able to adjust on the fly, but most can't.

So, take this point to heart. **Your audience is the key to your success, know them!**

Now that you know the audience you will be presenting to, it's time to write your speech.

Begin with an introduction that establishes who you are, what your purpose is, what you'll be talking about. Wait! **You should also write your introduction. Who knows better than you about you, than you?** Write out your introduction and give it to the Master of Ceremonies. You want this introduction upbeat and really high in excitement. Let's call it the "Oh Boy" factor. Write it in such a way that your audience is saying to them selves, oh boy, oh boy oh boy! **Anticipation generates excitement!**

Okay, back to the speech introduction. Why is the introduction important? An introduction is crucial to a speech because it generates interest about the subject and provides information and structure to the subject presented.

This may sound strange, but your introduction should contain an introduction, body and conclusion. Yeah, I know, what the heck are you talking about? Okay, check it out! You just had the Master of Ceremonies give you a big intro so you better "Bring It!"

Your intro should start out with an excited friendly greeting to your audience. Interject humor here is always a great place to start by putting your audience at ease. Also, advise them of the duration and its structure. Let your audience know if there is a designated time for questions or if you will be open to questions during your presentation.

I have found that if you are open to questions during your presentation, questions are normally premature and that question is addressed later as part of your presentation. To avoid wasting time for you and your audience, answer the people something like, "your question is addressed later in the presentation." It is better to advise your audience that there will be a period for open questions as part of your introduction. You may want to include a joke, anecdote, or interesting fact to grab the audience's attention. Caution in this area is advised! Know your audience! An opening joke, or whatever, is called a "Ho hum crasher". Properly delivered you will get the audience's attention and set them at ease. **Ya see, you're not the only one nervous.** Your introduction should make up about 10 to 15 percent of the total speech.

Now you need to write the body of your speech. **This is where you bring out the big guns!** First, you already know what the organizer wants to achieve, I hope. If not find out! Some brainstorming is required here to make sure the goals and objectives are known and achieved for the required subject.

Audiences tend to have a short attention span. So, in the body of your speech purposely insert "attention getter's" to keep the audience with you. Normally every 2 to 4 minutes with in your speech you should place these "attention getters".

There are several ways to accomplish this feat as you could simply change the inflection of your voice, throw in some humor, and make reference to one of your visual controls, whatever you feel would maintain the attention of your audience. The audience won't know you are using a technique on them, but at the end of your presentation you want your attendees to say, Wow! That time sure went by fast! Take out a piece of paper or white board and write down three to seven main points to be covered in the body of your speech. Prioritize them according to the importance and effectiveness of reaching the goals and objectives of your presentation. During this process, you might delete points that aren't crucial to your speech if you have too many for your time-frame or add additional points to meet your time requirements.

This is the area you dazzle them with your brilliance and perfection, yeah! Start with your most important point first. Then go to your least important point and move back toward the most important in the structure of the body. For example, if you have seven points with number 7 being the most important and number 1 being the least important, your presentation order should be 7-1-2-3-4.-5-6.

Add foundation to each point using statistics, examples, anecdotes, quotations, visual controls or other supporting material. This is where you have the great opportunity to generate excitement in your audience. **Gets your adrenalin smokin' here! This is the fun part. Get animated! This is the place that will make you or break you!**

This is the point where I recommend that you place your question and answers. Open the floor with a simple transition like: "Are there any questions on what has been presented so far today?" What not to ask is: "Do you have any questions?"

"Why," you ask? Real story - I used the "do you have any questions?" and I got "Are we going to be served lunch in here or what?" I realized two things here. First I didn't hit the presentation out of the park because the gentleman was thinking about food, not the subject being presented. Second, I asked an open-ended question which was not directed to the subject presented. **That simple question not subject matter related, pretty much destroyed what had been presented. Also, I did not know the answer to the question. Bottom line I blew it!**

Write a conclusion that summarizes each of your points, restates your main purpose and leaves the audience with a lasting impression. The conclusion should make up 5 to 10 percent of your speech. **My goal with every presentation is for my audience to walk out at the end and say only one word. Damn!**

One of the worst mistakes you can make as a public speaker is talking too long. Not only will you send some folks to la-la land, you will make some of them angry. It doesn't matter if your entire speech was outstanding and the audience came away with information that will change their lives. If you talk too long, they will leave saying, "That speaker just wouldn't shut-up!" Don't let this happen to you! Say what you have to say and sit down. Before you do, give them a well thought out conclusion

The last thing you say may be the most remembered. So, put as much time into creating and practicing your conclusion as you put into any other part of your presentation. Just like your introduction, your conclusion does not have to be humorous. It could be motivational, challenging, thoughtful, respectful of the length of the presentation, or it could restate your points in a different way. Make your conclusion have impact on what the audience takes home with them. Sometime during your presentation ask the audience to take some kind of action. Basically, do something specific as a result

of your presentation. If you haven't asked them to do something by now, the conclusion is your last chance to do so. You want your audience to really take an action requirement away with them and use the information they came away with.
If the subject is suitable, the use of a humorous conclusion works well. If you leave them laughing and applauding, they will leave with an extremely positive impression about you. If the subject is not appropriate to end with humor, you could end with facts or quotation that leaves the audience thoughtful and quiet. Even the most serious public speaking subjects can benefit from humor, but the humor should be used throughout the body of the presentation.

This same technique can be very effective in ending a mostly humorous speaking engagement. Have them laughing all along while you make your points. Then finish seriously. This contrast will create a great impact. It will convey the fact that you believe in a fun approach to the subject, but the results are serious to you.

Link your introduction, points and conclusions together with smooth transitions. Give them contact information if they have questions after the event. This is a good reason to have a forum on your website.

Chapter 19: Creating Your Speech

This chapter is where you learn to create your own speech, one step at a time. This chapter is important because it discusses and shows how you can come up with good content. Remember, good content dispels speech anxiety because it eliminates your fear of not knowing what to say.

Go through the steps and think about the examples given. As you do, endeavor to create a speech of your own.

Let's say that you are Amy Reich, HR Manager of Rimo Corporation, a company that specializes in creating and marketing arts and crafts products. On the company's 3rd anniversary celebration, you are asked to welcome the company's new employees, most of whom are fresh graduates, as part of the program. You are given 5-10 minutes for your message.

Step 1Determine the basic information you need

General Theme/Occasion: Welcoming new employees/ 3rd Anniversary Celebration

Speech Topic: Why Rimo Corp. is a great place to work.

Audience: Target audience will be the new employees of Rimo Corp., but will include more senior employees as well. About 80 individuals aged 18-45 years old.

Venue: Conference Hall

Speech Purpose: To motivate the new employees of Rimo Corp. by citing reasons as to why it is a great place to work.

Thesis Statement: There are three basic reasons why Rimo Corp. is a great place to work.

Step 2 Research

For a speech such as this, your research may include reviewing the company's website, history, and vision-mission. Since the speech is meant to inspire or motivate new employees, citing success stories will also be of great help. If you have a wonderful corporate video, show it. Photos of the company's events, and mementos of milestones and achievements may also be used.

Step 3 Create your main outline

The main outline is based on your thesis statement. For this example, the thesis statement limits you to three main points. Can you think of main points for this speech?

Step 4 Provide supporting evidence / examples

Once you have your three main points, you need to provide supporting evidence/examples that will substantiate each of your main points. Think about the main points you have enumerated earlier—what kind of examples/evidence will you need to support them? What pieces of information do you need to look for? For each main statement, try to give two supporting examples.

Step 5 Make the introduction of your speech

The introduction has two purposes: 1) to catch the attention of your audience and

2) to clarify the purpose of your speech. Try to write this down, word for word.

Step 6 Make the conclusion of your speech

The conclusion has two purposes 1) to signal that your speech has come to an end, and 2) to recap what you have discussed and show how you have achieved the purpose of your speech. As a bonus, the conclusion must also leave a memorable statement for your audience. You can also try to tie up your ending statement in the conclusion with your "attention statement" in the introduction. For example, if you chose to catch the attention of your audience in the introduction by asking a question, your conclusion may restate that question in the end, or provide the answer to it. Like the introduction, try to write the conclusion down, word for word.

Note that the example given for the speech is an "imaginary" company. For the purpose of this exercise, be as creative as you can and imagine what Rimo Corp. really is like. The objective is to help you determine what information you need to put in the body of your speech, in order to support your thesis statement and speech purpose.

Here is a sample speech based on the preceding steps discussed:

Introduction:

Good evening everyone. Take a look at this usual scenario that the new members of our company probably experience. A friend of them calls, and asks, "So where do you work?" "Rimo Corp," they answer. And the friend answers back - "Hmm... Rimo Corp... what's that?!"

Today we celebrate Rimo Corp's third anniversary. We are not as popular as other brands, but most of us, including myself, are very happy to be in this company, which is such a great place to work. To those of you who are new members of this family, of this corporation, we give you a warm, warm welcome, and we'd like to share with you three simple reasons as to why Rimo is such a great place to work.

First, we are built on passion.

The story of Ross and Keith, our company's young founders are all about their passion for the arts and crafts and how these bring people together (brief story on how they started the company)

Most of us in this company are happy to go to work, and because of that, we go the extra mile. Kent Miller, our Employee of the Month, went from being accounting manager to being the delivery guy for our client.

We value our people.

The company offers various perks and privileges.

We have scholarship programs.

We have quarterly awards to look forward to.

We have various opportunities for further learning, innovation, and promotion.

We are a small company, so we easily notice and promote performers.

We are a small company, so we can allocate our resources to ensure the development of **all**, not just **some** of the members of our company.

We make people happy.

We care about people—this is our job.

We have achieved 98% customer satisfaction rating in our evaluation this year (we must be doing something right!)

Our surveys show that eighty percent of our customers are return customers who have become loyal to our products and services.

We care about relationships

The messages of our art work are about family, love, and friendship.

We will continue to create more products and services that will bring people together and help make them happy.

Chapter 20: Body Language

Less than 10% of our communication is done with our words. Body language is therefore a huge part of interpersonal communication and a core element of a great presentation.

Great body language shows that you are relaxed, confident, assured, and composed. Don't underestimate how much people will judge you based on your physical comportment: how you hold yourself and move.

Below are the core elements for rock-solid body language and great physical presence onstage.

Be open with your arms and shoulders. Don't cross your arms. Don't put your hands in your pockets. It can, however, be OK to leave one hand in your pocket whilst you gesture with the other.

Stand up straight with relaxed shoulders. Definitely don't slouch forward. The best trick is to imagine a string going through your spine, out through the top of your head and directly up to the sky. Imagine that the string is taut and holding you perfectly vertical.

Use hand movements deliberately and regularly, but conservatively. Use gestures to express yourself, but don't try to overwhelm the content with excessive movements.

Imagine that you are talking to a group of friends about something you are confident and happy about. This relaxed, open, "happy" body language is what you want to transfer into your presentation.

Mute TED talks and other presenters on YouTube so that you can focus on how the presenters move and hold themselves. Follow the principles they follow, and imitate the odd gesture/technique if you can do it naturally.

Mute a video of yourself giving a talk and make notes on how you look. This may feel awkward, but it really is the only way to be fully conscious of how you hold yourself. Ask friends for feedback as well; if you're feeling brave, you can even post it on social media and ask for feedback there.

Ensure that you practice great posture and body language beforehand so that it is natural during your presentation. It is fine to take an occasional pause during a presentation to check your posture, but constantly being aware of your body is distracting—it will make you feel and appear uncomfortable.

As well as your body language being important to a great presentation, your clothes and style are important, too. It is essential that you look your best. People judge style and appearance—accept it. If you aren't fashion conscious, ask a stylish friend for some advice.

Practice, Practice, Practice

Probably the biggest secret to becoming a great presenter is to practice. This may sound obvious, but many overlook it. Some think, "How hard can it be to talk to a group of people? I talk to people all of the time, and I know the subject I'm presenting on in every detail!" Others think "I'm just not a public speaker, some people have 'it,' others don't, and I simply don't have 'it'."

However, few if any great public speakers are born that way, or are able to perform well just because they know the topic they are presenting on. **Everyone** needs to practice. And practice is what you have to do in order to be a great presenter, or even to give one good presentation.

Practicing your presenting skills is the only way to iron out all the gaps and weaknesses in the material you are going to present, and it is the only way to improve your presenting skillset generally.

Below are ideas on how to practice and how to get the most out of your practice sessions.

Feedback is essential. At first, record yourself and watch it again. Make changes and improvements based on the ideas you have learned in this book. Then, escalate to getting feedback from friends, family, and colleagues. Joining a local presenting group like Toastmasters is obviously an exceptional step to take if you can. Also, consider using online resources to upload videos of yourself. Use websites like Elance or Fiverr to find services that can give you feedback. These will vary in quality – you will have to pay more to get the best feedback.

Differentiate between sessions practicing the specific presentation you are working on, and practicing your presenting skillset more generally. In between giving presentations in your work/classes, try to work on your skillset so that you are sharp when it comes to future presentations. You can then work on making that specific presentation great, whilst already having good body language, eye contact, etc.

Find the time to practice your skillset can be difficult, so think of other "indirect" routes to improving your skills. For example, play guitar at open mic nights to practice being in front of a crowd, get a few shifts doing cold call sales to practice selling, or maybe become a tour guide at your local museum so that you can practice talking to small groups.

Create a strategy/process that integrates feedback and allows you to refine the presentation you are working on. This is especially helpful if you will be giving presentations on a regular basis. Your process might look like the following:

Plan my speech and what I am going to talk about

Draft my speech as best I can

Practice my speech in front of the mirror

Record myself on my smartphone, making corrections to the speech and how I present

Perform in front of friends and family to make sure I am confident

If Anything Goes Wrong, Don't Panic

If something goes wrong during your speech, don't panic. This is far from the endpoint, and it can even be spun to your advantage. The characteristic of vulnerability is deeply endearing. If in the overwhelming moment of trying to give an amazing presentation, you skip through ideas in the wrong order, or perhaps the technology you are using breaks down, just relax into the situation. Sure, be a little annoyed but don't get overwhelmed, also laugh if it makes sense to.

Even if it seems a little too optimistic, try to see a mistake as a positive, and just move on. Consider the following potential "re-frames" to make this shift in mindset:

It's interesting — an event to grab the audience's attention. Something going wrong might bring people back into being engaged with your message.

You show yourself to be fallible, vulnerable, and a little more likable—and being likable is half the game. If you're likeable, the audience is going to want to take your ideas on board.

The audience is perhaps entertained, so again, they are a little more engaged mentally. If you've laughed about it or made a joke, it might be still more entertaining. That doesn't mean that you should turn it into a circus act, but if it seems natural don't be afraid to laugh a little.

That's not to say that you want to self-sabotage aspects of your presentation just to make them more interesting, vulnerable, and entertaining. But if something does go a little (or a lot) wrong, there is an opportunity there to in fact make your presentation even better – it all depends on how you react.

This leads to another important idea: the audience wants you to do well. They want to be entertained, educated, and swept away into an interesting story. Depending on the situation, they may even be really rooting for you (for example, if everyone knows you are doing your first presentation, they're going to want you to do well). So don't think of the audience as an enemy that has to be fought and overcome. Just give them every reason to like you, like what you have to say, and really "get" the message you are trying to convey.

You should also consider the importance of humour in your presentation. Of course, you should be aware of the tone and what is expected from you, but you can let yourself have fun and share a joke if it makes sense. You could even consider making a joke about your lack of experience in giving presentations. Say something like, "Hi, I'm new to this presentation game, and I've been up all night watching Steve Jobs on YouTube in preparation."

Lightening the mood can be the best way to get over being nervous, because you no longer have to fight the nervousness internally. It can be incredibly stressful to try and appear perfect at something when you aren't. By calling yourself out a little, you'll feel more relaxed.

Chapter 21: Talk About Subjects The Audience Can Relate To

Whenever I speak in public, I am astounded by just how effective speaking about subjects the audience can relate to can be.

It may not make or break a talk or presentation, but it can certainly give it a powerful edge. Aiming for too much of a niche can be risky unless you are at a high level and know exactly what you are doing.

Where possible, it is a great idea to do your research on subjects the majority of the audience is likely to be knowledgeable about, and they will thank you for it.

For example, a few months ago, I read a poem I had written on a hypothetical world in which superstition did not exist, and as proud as I was of what I had written, it was not nearly as much of a universal crowd-pleaser as subjects which were more relatable to the majority of the audience.

Subjects which are generally well-received include: journeys on public transport, awkward conversations, cycling, dancing and public speaking itself.

In humorous speeches or stand-up comedy, the subject of working in retail or catering tends to go down well, as this is something many people have done at some point in their lives.

Other subjects that are generally well-received, due to their relatability, are: family, friends, relationships, school, work, driving and holidays.

However, bear in mind that any one of the subjects listed above could be sensitive for particular individuals in the audience, for a myriad of reasons. You should therefore tread carefully in terms of the length you linger on any particular subject, or the detail you go into.

For example, if someone in the audience has just lost a family member in a car accident, it may not be the best idea to spend too long discussing family days out in the car. Always try to be sensitive to what the audience may or may not wish to hear talked about, and be prepared to drop a subject at a moment's notice if necessary.

One of the most effective subjects of all is the city, town or local area in which you are giving your talk, as this is one of the most likely subjects for a large proportion of those present to have intimate knowledge of.

This is especially easy, and effective, if the talk you are delivering is somewhere you currently live, have lived previously or have visited a lot. In this case, you are likely to have at least a moderately detailed knowledge of it, its ins and outs and its quirky idiosyncrasies which locals can relate to.

This includes details about a place as it was many years ago, which seasoned local residents in your audience may remember, for example a shop or local business that was close to your heart that was forced to shut down. In these cases, it is likely that someone present may share your views.

Even if the talk you are giving does not directly relate to this place, the odd reference to it here and there can do wonders when it comes to connecting with your audience.

If the event you are speaking at is somewhere you speak regularly, or have spoken at in the past, you could draw on your experience and talk about specific details of the venue which your audience may be familiar with, especially if they frequent it regularly.

You should also avoid subjects which could be offensive or particularly contentious. Some speakers may be tempted to try to be a bit edgy with their subject matter. However, this can be risky, and my advice would be to err on the side of caution in this respect. If mentioning a contentious subject is unavoidable, it is best not to do so in an opinionated way.

Chapter 22: Preparing Your Speech

You are now ready to prepare your speech.Yes, there was a lot of work that you had to do before finally reaching this step, but it was well worth it.Now that you have taken a hard look at your fears and started to develop a more positive mindset, you are in a much better frame of mind to prepare a successful speech.You also have given careful consideration of what the main goal is for your speech, and you have a clear idea of who your audience is and what the setting will be for your presentation.With all this in mind, it is time to prepare your speech.

The first and most important thing to keep in mind is that you are not going to want to write a speech that you read word by word.It is almost always a bad idea to read a written speech at the podium or standing in front of a group.Instead, you want to prepare notes that you can refer to, including an outline and brief examples to help keep you on track.

Brain Dump

The first step is to just get all of your thoughts out on paper without thinking about the right order or anything else.Just get everything out on paper.Keep doing this until you have more than enough material for your speech.

Research

Review your notes from the brain dump and figure out if there is any research you need to ensure that what you say in your speech is accurate.Find your answers by doing research at the library or online, consulting with colleagues or checking your own resources.

Prepare An Outline

The next step in the process is to prepare an outline of your speech.You will want to have some supporting data or references that back each point.Examples or stories are very good ways to illustrate your points.Keep your time frame in mind when preparing outline.You will obviously need a much longer outline for a half hour speech than a 10 minute talk.When you are practicing your speech you will be able to check to make sure you are staying within your time frame.

Fill In The Details

Review your outline and make sure it is relevant and supports the main goal you are trying to achieve with your speech.When you are filling in your details, try to use interesting examples, stories and some humor to add interest.Just keep in mind that these need to be brief.The last thing you want to do is tell a long, rambling story.You don't have time for that.You want short, memorable examples.

Introduction

Make sure to have an interesting and compelling introduction that really draws the audience in.You want to have an interesting hook that creates excitement and interest.Prepare your audience for what you are about to tell them. Having a strong introduction is key to a successful speech. It can help get the audience engaged, set the proper expectations and prepare people for the rest of your speech and how it ties in with your goal.

Body

Here is where you will provide your "bullet points," along with examples that support your goal. Guide your audience every step of the way. Be interesting, informative and entertaining.

A successful conclusion will wrap up all the themes of your speech and tie them to your goal. You will want to summarize the key takeaways of your speech and leave your audience with a call to action that compels them to do something that supports your goal.

Remember that your goal is not to have a perfectly written speech that you can read word for word. Rather, you are preparing an outline with brief notes to keep you on track and jog your memory. You will continue to perfect your speech during your upcoming practice sessions.

Chapter 23: What To Speak About

Now that we have covered the easy three-step dance formula, the alarm bells may be going off inside you - what to speak about?

For a lot of people who have mustered the courage to begin this journey, this becomes the sixty-four million dollar question.

What will I talk about?

In the next part of this book, I give you a whole bunch of ideas on what to speak about. You may find it easier than you thought to come up with something! You might even say **"Hey I have a story that would be great"**.

Below is a list of subjects that may help you discover a person, an event or story that will get you started.

You may have already thought of a 'ripping yarn' (a term used in journalism for a great story) that you could work up into a really engaging 'speak'.

If so, fantastic.

searching or deciding on "what could I speak about"

Choose a subject you are already PASSIONATE about.

PASSION is a magic ingredient that helps you get past any fear you may have about speaking.

Like the mother whose son was killed by a drunk driver - she started an entire movement via a campaign to increase the penalties and bring national awareness to the issue. She became a passionate speaker almost by default.

She probably never saw herself as a powerful and inspirational speaker. However, because of her commitment and sheer force of will to do something about drunk drivers, the voice in her just emerged.

There are countless examples of ordinary people becoming extraordinary speakers because some issue moved them to action. They became PASSIONATE.

When you are truly passionate about something, whether it be a life issue, an environmental concern, a hobby that has turned into a business, an idea about a campaign or simply a passion you want share with others, it will serve you if you let it.

Question. Why does a simple video of an animal being cute or funny go viral on the net?

Why does anything go viral on the net?

Because it entertains, tugs at the heart strings, rattles the funny bone or simply grabs your attention because it's so weird, so random or so shocking!

A video going viral on the net or even a single picture being shared millions of times just shows what appeals to people.

Are YOU attracted by inspirational stories?
Most of us are.

If you are looking for inspiration to work up a 'speak' that will really 'move' your audience, start
with a story about someone or something that truly inspires YOU.

To beat the challenge of "I don't know what to speak about" ... ask yourself this question.

Who do you know that has a really moving, heroic, weird, amazing or life-changing story?

Do you know someone who was involved in a rescue of some kind - especially one that had a happy ending?

Do you admire someone who started something like a charity, a foundation, a house for wayward kids, an animal shelter, an environmental project or movement of some kind?

The 9/11 tragedy is literally peppered with people who rose above their own safety to help others. These types of stories will definitely be emotion-charged. It's been a long time, in terms of years since that catastrophic event, yet the emotions and people connected to it are still very fresh in our memories.

Is there anyone in the military you know who served overseas and lived to tell of their experiences?Perhaps you? A spouse or partner, brother, sister, uncle?

This of course needs to be within the boundaries of national security. That won't stop stories of life-long friendships made. Of how life was on base or in camp. Of places you got to know or visit. How everyone coped.How difficult it was missing family and friends. Etc.

Do you know anyone, or a group or 'people power' movement that has saved an historic building that was destined for the wrecking ball?

Are you aware of a young person who bravely put themselves in danger to save someone?

Is there someone in your community who has done amazing work and not really been recognized for it?

Haiti has been battered by severe weather events that ripped through towns and villages, leaving a trail of devastation - are there stories of survival that you know about or experienced yourself?

Have you seen random acts of kindness and stories of paying-it-forward that audiences would like to know about?

Do you have an animal that is close to you or maybe saved you from some kind of life threatening situation? Animal stories are universal in their appeal. Again videos of animals doing unusual, funny or whacky things are the ones that go viral on the net. A great clue.

Is there someone you know, perhaps you who has overcome a life threatening illness that would inspire others to keep going under drastic circumstances? Again, many of these are highly emotional stories which adds to its appeal. Especially if there is a happy ending!

Has someone guided you or mentored you in some way that completely changed the course of your life for the better?

Have you risen above the dark days of drug use and lived to tell the tale and are now helping others to do the same? Or how you got out of the cycle or the 'trap' of that lifestyle.

And the list goes on and on.

Look around you.

What event, person, and act of bravery, lucky escape or disaster have you survived, know of or helped someone else get through?

Have you been on some travel adventure that would make a great story? The road less traveled has high appeal amongst audiences.

Have you, or know someone who has risen above and beyond the call of duty in some way?

Is there someone you know who has beaten all the odds to keep living and enjoying life?

It could be about the city you live in - all the great cities of the world have wonderful back stories. Do you know one?

As life changes in this world of ours, stories about how 'things used to be' will be interesting to some people.

Have you traveled to another country and discovered something about the people of that land that would make for great listening?

Do you know someone who would be considered 'ordinary' yet has done something extraordinary with their life?

Is there something great you want to do in your life, but never had the chance to do?

Find someone who has maybe done what YOU would like to be able to do, talk to them and make a story to tell.

What do you do in your spare time, or for the sheer fun of it?

Do you go running/jogging in the park to keep fit and managed to stick with your routine to lose an extraordinary amount of weight?

Do you build model planes, drones with cameras and fly them on the weekend?

Do you like taking movies with your go-pro on the end of your surfboard, skateboard or snowboard?

Maybe the whole go-pro thing on a helmet-cam for biking, skiing, rock climbing, skydiving or some other adventure sport where you end up with great pieces of vision. Using vision in your story is a GREAT idea if it helps you relax and tell the story even better. This means you can include video clips in your speak!

Do you collect something unusual?

Do you fix things, like on American Restoration?

Are you a motor person - tinkering with other mechanical stuff?

Do you ride/buy/sell/fix/collect/restore motorcycles or automobiles?

Are you interested in, own or restore Muscle Cars or classics from the 50-60's? (Ever been to Cuba?)

Do you go hiking, climbing or do survival stuff?

Are you a weapons person - handguns, target shooting, range shooting, and hunting?

Are you a gardener who grows special varieties of plants or a new variety of roses?

Do you paint, draw, sketch, sculpt, build stuff from metal or wood, do you go sailing, love history, travel, love trains, planes or automobiles or do you have kids that do something different?

Pheeeeew.

Everybody does something, even if you are a SOCCER mum who coaches her kid's local team, there is a story in there somewhere!

Here is an example of a person I met many years ago who really inspires me. Her name is HFH ... a mother of two and a tireless worker for charity who has spent her whole life helping others.

Eight years ago, her husband developed a life-threatening illness and unfortunately passed away.A year later, she had a massive stroke. That was followed by a whole year in rehab. She was left with one arm hanging uselessly by her side, calipers on her legs and only able to move about six inches with each step.

Now?

This woman is back to being a whirlwind of activity in helping others - in different ways and

certainly at a different speed. She cooks one handed ... there is a book on the way on "How to

cook with one hand while the other one just hangs in there!" Give up? No way.

She is the kindest and most loving friend. To say she has been an inspiration to me does not really cover it. HFH was recently named "Citizen of the year" in her own city.

Do you know of anyone who has overcome the odds to keep playing the game of life?

There are plenty of them out there. Some become well known through their attitude and their deeds while others stay in the background with their story untold.

If you are looking for inspiration, just look around you.

When you are looking for something, you will generally find it. Some people are

inspired by their mothers or fathers. Some of us are inspired by our children. Some of us are inspired by our siblings.
What and who inspires you?
A great place to start looking.

"What will I talk about"?
As we all know, life deals some pretty tough cards at times but it also deals out great, amazing and inspirational ones too.
I truly hope that this section of the book has given you plenty of meat on the bone in terms of discovering something to speak about.
So go ahead on your search for 'what I will speak about?'
You may just go from 'I can't think of anything' to 'Wow guess what I just thought of to speak about'?

So start making notes on subjects, people, events or anything that pops up as a result of the list above. You may even want to speak about YOU.

In the next bit of the book, we are going to start writing these ideas down in slightly more detail firstly, then go on with how to whip the ideas into shape.

Are you up for that?

Let's go for a summary of
what we do know so far.

We know the number one fear in America and many other parts of the world is PUBLIC SPEAKING.

We know that fear is mostly irrational, meaning IT'S ALL IN YOUR HEAD!

We know that when overcoming a fear, it's generally not knowing what to do and all the

WHAT IF'S your brain can come up with.

We do know that when you break it down into small sections, at least it gives you a clear understanding of WHAT TO DO, HOW TO DO IT and WHAT TO PRACTICE.

We do know that once you know all these things/facts, the paralyzing fear of speaking in public, is slowly replaced with

CONFIDENCE based on at the very least, a little bit of good old fashioned know how.

We do know that when you go through the big list above, that you will or most likely come up with something YOU CAN TALK ABOUT.

We do know that if you persist, you might even enjoy putting it together with the Three-step dance of OPEN, BODY CLOSE.

And we do know this formula works because it's the simple version of how the professionals do it.

Now it's time to capture ideas and choose one, or several possibilities for YOU.

Chapter 24: Dealing With Problems

- Introduction
- The NPD rule
- Putting problems in perspective
- The PBD rule
- Taking time to deal with problems
- How to cope with a technology disaster!
- Preventing failures
- Dealing with any unexpected issues
- Dealing with difficult people
- Maintaining your 'Alpha' position
- Section Review

In a perfect world there would never be any problems: projectors would never break down, people would never ask difficult questions and there would never be any unexpected issues.

Unfortunately, no matter of training and experience can totally prevent problems occurring, however you can certainly take a number of steps to ensure that, if you do encounter an issue, you can manage it without it totally disrupting your presentation.

There are two rules you can use when you have a problem during a presentation, the first is the

NPD rule

NPD = No Permanent Damage

The first rule tells us that we should keep things in perspective. Basically, giving a presentation is considerably less dangerous than a number of other activities (for example: flying a plane, mining or lion taming). We should always remember that, within reason, whatever you do or whatever happens will not cause permanent damage to either you or your audience.

It is worth remembering NPD because you can sometimes feel that the world is about to end when you are giving a presentation and something goes wrong. You are in the spotlight in front of an audience who are all waiting to see how you deal with the situation.

The unexpected can happen to anyone. The difference between the embarrassing moments (for both the audience and the speaker) and memorable moments when something goes wrong are the presenter. You can turn a problem into an opportunity. For example, if the projector fails use this as a chance to show how well you know your subject and just carry on without slides. If you have rehearsed and have your cue cards ready, I can assure you that any audience will forget the problem and be overtaken by admiration with how you dealt with it.

This is when the second rule comes into play...

The PBD Rule

The second rule we need to keep in mind while presenting is the PBD rule: **PBD = Pause, Breathe, Deal with it**

Take an example: you are in the middle of a presentation when suddenly the projector stops working – what is your immediate reaction? If it is to panic or become flustered, then this will become obvious for the audience and it will start a spiral of nerves which you may not recover from in the presentation. If it is to immediately and publicly blame the technical staff you will make yourself look bad in the eyes of the audience – I can assure you no technician plans for these things to happen!

What you should do is:

- Pause
  o Take a moment to weigh up the options.
- Breathe
  o If you remember what we said about breathing when dealing with presentation nerves. Taking a deep breath can start to calm you.
- Deal with it
  o You need to carry on or, if that is impossible, take control of the room.

As we said on the last page, you can turn a problem into an opportunity. There is nothing worse than watching a presenter flounder when there is a problem. If you take a moment you can come back stronger than ever!

Dealing with a technology disaster

One of the most common things to go wrong involves technology, and computers in particular! It is all too common to see someone struggling with a computer or tablet moments before a presentation or to have the audience treated to the desktop and a search for the correct file.

The best way to prevent an issue with technology is to prepare before the event and to ensure you have an opportunity to test your presentation and equipment before you have to start speaking. There are a number of common issues which can occur. For example:

- When using your own PC with a projector there is no image displayed.
- When using a supplied PC you find that videos or sound files do not run correctly or that fonts and pictures are incorrect.

Before you give a presentation ensure that you have it backed up on a memory stick or online and ensure that you have saved all the required files (such as video and audio files) as well. If you are using your own laptop make sure you know how to switch on the external monitor output, otherwise the projector will not be able to show your presentation – there is usually a key combination you need to press to get this to work.

Also make sure you go through every slide checking for errors; sometimes different machines can show pictures etc. in different ways. It is important to be sure that diagrams have not been altered and also check that any videos are working (you may need to ask for a sound connection to the public address system and adjust the volume on your machine).If you check all of these items you will eliminate 99% of any issues you may encounter, leaving you with what are mostly very unlikely problems that are out of your hands.

You may want to consider creating a new 'Presentation' user on your device which has no email or other applications. This can be used to deliver presentations with no notifications or annoying pop-ups!

Dealing with difficult people

We have covered preparing for your presentation and ensuring that you have the right content for the audience, however sometimes no matter what you do there will be someone who has another agenda or just wishes to be difficult.

It is very rare that you have to deal with difficult people in a presentation. If you do have to, however, the most important thing to remember is that you have to maintain your Alpha Presenter status. By this I mean that you need to be sure that you do not give control of your audience to the individual.

Firstly, follow the PBD rule: take a breath and respond politely to their issue or concern. Remember that you should listen to their comment when you can (don't allow them to go on, but make an effort to show that you are not just preventing their input). You will need to be forceful but do not try to get into an argument from the lectern. If there is a response you can give do so, if they choose to come back and argue suggest that they take the matter up with you after the presentation. It is impossible to try and have a two- way conversation at the cost of the rest of the audience.

In the most extreme situation when they will not stop arguing you need to stop the presentation until there is order. Apologise to the audience and either blank the screen (hit the B key on your keyboard in PowerPoint to toggle a black screen) or step off the stage. This is extreme; however, it shows that you will not be undermined by the individual.

Remember however that this is a very rare situation and you may never need this advice.

Section Review

In this section we learnt how to deal with issues. We have:

- put problems in perspective with the No Permanent Damage rule
- learnt how to get time to deal with an issue with the Pause, Breathe, Deal with it rule
- learnt how to cope with a technology disaster
- learnt how to deal with difficult people.

In the next section we will look at how you can improve your audience dynamics.

Conclusion

The main elements that are emphasized here are to:
· Calm down and control your breathing
· Use "Power Posing" to get your body in the right state
· Be comfortable with the specific topic or problem you are talking about
· Use your voice as a powerful instrument to act out your message
· Practice, practice, practice!
· Be yourself---because you're always GREAT at being yourself.

Congratulations on completing this guide! You are on your way to becoming an effective public speaker. Continue to get education and practice. Look at other speakers such as the speakers from "TED" on YouTube.

Notice the way that they open their speech and how they deliver the message. They also use their body, gestures and voice to relate to their audience.

www.ingramcontent.com/pod-product-compliance
Lightning Source LLC
Chambersburg PA
CBHW072007070526
44583CB00015B/1373